守護霊インタビュー

駐日アメリカ大使
キャロライン・ケネディ
日米の新たな架け橋

INTERVIEWING
THE GUARDIAN SPIRIT OF
U.S. AMBASSADOR
CAROLINE KENNEDY

大川隆法
RYUHO OKAWA

守護霊インタビュー 駐日アメリカ大使
キャロライン・ケネディ
日米の新たな架け橋

Interviewing the Guardian Spirit of
U.S. Ambassador Caroline Kennedy
A New Bridge Between Japan and the U.S.

Preface

We Japanese love "Mr. President" Kennedy. We are fascinated by his "Captain America" like heroism. And also, he was a tragic hero. His life became American legend itself. Here in Japan, we've luckily accepted his legendary daughter Caroline Kennedy as the new U.S. Ambassador. This decision might be the best one of President Obama's performance. We hope Carol become a new bridge between Japan and the U.S.

This little book will be helpful to both Carol and Japanese people, I hope.

February 14, 2014

National Teacher and World Teacher

Master & CEO of Happy Science Group

Ryuho Okawa

はじめに

　日本人なら「大統領」といえば、ケネディ好きときたもんだ。私たちは、彼の「キャプテン・アメリカ」的な英雄気質に憧れる。しかも悲劇のヒーローだからたまんない。ケネディの人生そのものがアメリカの伝説そのものなのだ。ここ日本では、幸運にも、これまた伝説的なケネディの娘、キャロライン・ケネディを新駐日大使として迎え入れることができた。

　オバマ大統領の決定としては、最高傑作の１つだろう。

　日本人たちは、キャロルが日米の新たな架け橋となることを願ってやまない。

　この小著が、キャロルと日本人同胞の導きとなることを、私は心底願うものである。

2014年2月14日

国師 兼 世界教師

幸福の科学グループ創始者兼総裁

大川隆法

Contents

Preface 2

1 Caroline's Guardian Spirit Makes an "Informal"Appearance 14

2 Her View on Japan-U.S. and Japan-China Relations 36

3 True Emotions Behind America's Disappointment in Yasukuni Visit 54

4 World War II 74

5 Comfort Women Issue and Women's Rights... 100

6 The Reason Behind the Kennedy Tragedies ... 114

7 Drive-hunt Dolphin Killing, and Japanese vs. American Cultures 126

目　次

はじめに 3

1 キャロライン守護霊「非公式に」登場 15

2 日米・日中関係をどう見るか 37

3 米国が靖国参拝に「失望」の真意は 55

4 第二次世界大戦をどう考えるか 75

5 慰安婦問題と女性の権利について 101

6 ケネディ家の悲劇の理由 115

7 イルカ漁と日米文化の違い 127

8 Japanese Princess and Roman Emperor in
    Past Lives?....................................... 150

9 Message to Japan 166

8 過去世は日本の姫やローマ皇帝か 151

9 日本へのメッセージ 167

This book is the transcript of spiritual messages given by the guardian spirit of U.S. Ambassador to Japan, Caroline Kennedy.

These spiritual messages were channeled through Ryuho Okawa. However, please note that because of his high level of enlightenment, his way of receiving spiritual messages is fundamentally different from other psychic mediums who undergo trances and are completely taken over by the spirits they are channeling.

Each human soul is made up of six soul siblings, one of whom acts as the guardian spirit of the person living on earth. People living on earth are connected to their guardian spirits at the innermost subconscious level. They are a part of people's very souls and therefore, exact reflections of their thoughts and philosophies.

It should be noted that these spiritual messages are opinions of the individual spirits and may contradict the ideas or teachings of the Happy Science Group.

The spiritual messages and questions were spoken in English.

本書は、駐日アメリカ大使キャロライン・ケネディ守護霊の霊言を収録したものである。

　「霊言現象」とは、あの世の霊存在の言葉を語り下ろす現象のことをいう。これは高度な悟りを開いた者に特有のものであり、「霊媒現象」（トランス状態になって意識を失い、霊が一方的にしゃべる現象）とは異なる。

　また、人間の魂は6人のグループからなり、あの世に残っている「魂の兄弟」の1人が守護霊を務めている。つまり、守護霊は、実は自分自身の魂の一部である。

　したがって、「守護霊の霊言」とは、いわば、本人の潜在意識にアクセスしたものであり、その内容は、その人が潜在意識で考えていること（本心）と考えてよい。

　ただ、「霊言」は、あくまでも霊人の意見であり、幸福の科学グループとしての見解と矛盾する内容を含む場合がある点、付記しておきたい。

　なお、今回、霊人や質問者の発言は英語にて行われた。本書は、それに日本語訳を付けたものである。

Interviewing the Guardian Spirit of U.S. Ambassador Caroline Kennedy
A New Bridge Between Japan and the U.S.

February 8, 2014
at Master's Holy Temple: Sacred Shrine of Great Enlightenment, Taigokan
Happy Science, Tokyo
Spiritual Messages from the Guardian Spirit of Caroline Kennedy

守護霊インタビュー 駐日アメリカ大使 キャロライン・ケネディ 日米の新たな架け橋

2014年2月8日　東京都・幸福の科学 教祖殿 大悟館にて
キャロライン・ケネディ守護霊の霊言

Caroline Bouvier Kennedy (1957-)

The daughter of the 35th President of the United States of America, John F. Kennedy. Currently, the U.S. ambassador to Japan. She attracted attention from around the world as the daughter of the president. After the assassination of President Kennedy, the family moved to New York. She received her Bachelor of Arts from Radcliffe College (became a part of Harvard University in 1999). She got married in 1986, and has two daughters and a son. In 1988, she received a Juris Doctor from Columbia Law School. She is an advisor to the Harvard Institute of Politics, as well as being active in numerous non-profit organizations. In 2008 U.S. presidential election, she showed her support to Barack Obama and attracted media attention. She has no experience as a politician, but through strong trust from President Obama, she was appointed the first female U.S. ambassador to Japan in November 2013.

Interviewers from Happy Science

Masashi Ishikawa
 Deputy Chief Secretary, First Secretarial Division /
 Chief of Overseas Missionary Work Promotion Office
 Religious Affairs Headquarters

Yuki Wada
 Manager, Overseas Missionary Work Promotion Office
 Religious Affairs Headquarters

Ai Saito
 Executive Director / Chief Secretary, First Secretarial
 Division / Advisor of Study Promotion Office
 Religious Affairs Headquarters

※ Interviewers are listed in the order that they appear in the transcript.
 Their professional titles represent their positions at the time of the interview.

キャロライン・ブーヴィエ・ケネディ（1957 －）

第35代アメリカ合衆国大統領ジョン・F・ケネディの長女で、現在、駐日アメリカ合衆国大使。大統領の娘として世界的な関心を集めるが、ケネディの暗殺後は一家でニューヨークに移住。名門ラドクリフ大学（1999年にハーバード大学と統合）では美術学の学士号を取得した。1986年に結婚して、2女1男をもうける。88年にコロンビア大学ロースクールで法学位を取得。ハーバード大学ケネディ・スクールの顧問などのほか、様々な慈善活動に関わってきた。2008年の大統領選挙ではバラク・オバマ候補への支持を表明し、メディアの注目を集めた。政治家としての実績はないが、オバマ大統領からの信頼が厚く、2013年11月、女性初の駐日米国大使に就任した。

質問者（幸福の科学）

石川雅士（宗務本部第一秘書局担当局長
　　　　兼 海外伝道推進室長）

和田ゆき（宗務本部海外伝道推進室チーフ）

斉藤愛　（理事 兼 宗務本部第一秘書局長
　　　　兼 学習推進室顧問）

※質問順。役職は収録当時のもの。

1 Caroline's Guardian Spirit Makes an "Informal" Appearance

Ryuho Okawa Today, I would like to summon the new ambassador from the U.S.A. known as Caroline Kennedy, the famous daughter of President Kennedy. We want to ask her guardian spirit about her opinion regarding Japanese matters and of other foreign countries, her own discipline of her real life, about the Kennedy family, and so on.

OK, this is the first time and first try for me (to conduct the spiritual messages of the guardian spirit of Caroline Kennedy). I don't exactly know if this will be successful or not, but we want to have a challenging spirit regarding this matter. Even for her, this must be her first experience, so she might also have an attention regarding this spiritual type of investigation.

Thinking in her terms, this might be a very hard test as an ambassador from the U.S.A., because we are trying to get her real thinking and real opinion. This is very

1　キャロライン守護霊「非公式に」登場

大川隆法　今日は、新しい米国大使でケネディ大統領の有名な娘さんの、キャロライン・ケネディを呼んでみたいと思います。彼女の守護霊に、日本や諸外国の問題についての意見、実生活における信条やケネディ家のことなども聞いてみたいと思います。

　さて、私にとって（キャロライン守護霊の霊言は）初回であり、初めての試みです。うまくいくかどうか、はっきりとは分かりませんが、これに関してはチャレンジ精神を持ちたいですね。彼女にとっても、これは初めての経験のはずですから、こうした霊的な形での調査に関心を持ってくれるかもしれません。

　彼女の立場を考慮すると、これは、米国大使として非常に〝厳しい試験〟になるかもしれません。私たちは彼女の真意や本音を引き出そうとしているからです。非常にきついことです。彼

hard. She can hide her real opinion and give an ordinary speech as an ambassador, but here, in Happy Science, that's very difficult. Today's interview will be very hard and interviewers are severe, so she will be frightened by very serious questions. There may be a lot of arrow-like questions from you (the interviewers).

She may even go back to the United States of America in the near future or even within a year if this interview is published in Japan. We don't have enough responsibility regarding her future, but we will try our best.

Ishikawa Within a year?

Ryuho Okawa (Laughs) I don't know exactly, but we will try. This might be her first experience, so it's very difficult for her. Please start kindly and lightly. Is that OK?

Let's begin. I will try to summon the guardian spirit of the ambassador, Ms. Kennedy. Are you willing to come over here, to Taigokan? Could you kindly speak to us

1 キャロライン守護霊「非公式に」登場

女は大使としては、自分の本音を隠して通常のスピーチをすることはできますが、ここ幸福の科学では、それは非常に難しいことです。本日のインタビューはとてもハードでしょうし、インタビュアーたちも〝厳しい〟ですから、非常に「重大な質問」をされて恐れをなすことでしょう。あなたがた（質問者）から矢のような質問がたくさん浴びせられるでしょうから。

　このインタビューが日本で出版されたら、彼女は近いうちに、あるいは１年以内にもアメリカに帰ってしまうかもしれませんね。彼女の将来に関して十分責任は持てませんが、できるだけ、がんばってみましょう。

石川　１年以内ですか？

大川隆法　（笑）はっきりとは分かりませんが、やってみましょう。初めての経験でしょうから、彼女にとっても非常に難しいでしょうね。どうか優しく軽い感じで始めてください。よろしいでしょうか。

　では始めましょう。ケネディ大使の守護霊をお呼びします。ここ大悟館にいらしていただけますでしょうか。政治や外交や日本の人々に関する本音や、ご自身のお考え、お

17

1 Caroline's Guardian Spirit Makes an "Informal" Appearance

your real opinion regarding politics, diplomacy, and on Japanese people? Or your own thinking, your memory about your father, or your opinion about the United States and other countries surrounding Japan – like China, South Korea, North Korea, Russia and other countries?

Ms. Caroline Kennedy, would you come down here? The guardian spirit of Ms. Caroline Kennedy, would you come down…

(Summons her guardian spirit)
(About 20 seconds of silence)

Caroline's guardian spirit resists revealing her true intention

Caroline Kennedy's Guardian Spirit* Hmm… (takes two deep breaths)

Ishikawa Hello.

Caroline's G.S. Huh?

*Caroline Kennedy's Guardian Spirit will be noted as Caroline's G.S. from this point on.

1 キャロライン守護霊「非公式に」登場

父上の思い出、また、米国や、日本を取り巻く中国・韓
国・北朝鮮・ロシアなどの国、その他の国々に対する、ご
意見をお聞かせいただけますでしょうか。

　キャロライン・ケネディさん、どうかおいでください。
キャロライン・ケネディさんの守護霊よ、どうかおいで
ください……。

(招霊する)
(約20秒間の沈黙)

真意をガードするキャロライン守護霊

キャロライン・ケネディ守護霊（以下「キャロライン守
護霊」）　うーん……（二回深く息を吐く）。

石川　こんにちは。

キャロライン守護霊　ん？

1 Caroline's Guardian Spirit Makes an "Informal" Appearance

Ishikawa Are you the United States ambassador to Japan, Ms. Caroline Kennedy?

Caroline's G.S. Yes.

Ishikawa The guardian spirit?

Caroline's G.S. Yes, of course.

Ishikawa OK.

Caroline's G.S. Oh, oh. What? What? It's a studio.

Ishikawa This place is one of the Headquarters of Happy Science.

Caroline's G.S. Happy Science! Famous Happy Science?

1　キャロライン守護霊「非公式に」登場

石川　駐日米国大使のキャロライン・ケネディさんですか。

キャロライン守護霊　ええ。

石川　守護霊ですか。

キャロライン守護霊　ええ、もちろんです。

石川　はい。

キャロライン守護霊　あら、あら、何？　何？　（ここは）スタジオですね。

石川　ここは、幸福の科学の本部の一つです。

キャロライン守護霊　幸福の科学！　あの有名な幸福の科学？

1 Caroline's Guardian Spirit Makes an "Informal" Appearance

Ishikawa Oh, do you know?

Caroline's G.S. Very famous! Very famous.

Ishikawa Oh, really? Thank you very much.

Caroline's G.S. Only in Japan (laughs).

Ishikawa (Laughs) I'm sorry. Today we would like to conduct a spiritual interview.

Caroline's G.S. Oh, spiritual interview?

Ishikawa Yes. Do you understand?

Caroline's G.S. Hmm…

Ishikawa You are the guardian spirit of Ms. Caroline Kennedy?

1　キャロライン守護霊「非公式に」登場

石川　えっ、ご存じなんですか。

キャロライン守護霊　とても有名ですよ！　とても有名。

石川　ほんとうですか。ありがとうございます。

キャロライン守護霊　日本でだけですけど（笑）。

石川　（笑）すみません。今日は、守護霊インタビューをさせていただきたいと思います。

キャロライン守護霊　ああ、守護霊インタビュー？

石川　はい。お分かりですか。

キャロライン守護霊　うーん……。

石川　キャロライン・ケネディさんの守護霊でいらっしゃいますよね。

1 Caroline's Guardian Spirit Makes an "Informal" Appearance

Caroline's G.S. I can understand the meaning, but I cannot prospect the influence of this interview (laughs). It is not an official one, you know? It is neither an official nor a classified interview, right?

Ishikawa This is not an official statement, but your true intention or true thoughts will be revealed.

Caroline's G.S. No, no. You can only *guess* true intention.

Ishikawa OK. Can we start?

Caroline's G.S. All right.

There is no problem in Japan

Ishikawa I think you are the only living child of the slain President J.F. Kennedy.

Caroline's G.S. "Child!"

キャロライン守護霊　意味は分かりますけど、このインタビューが及ぼす影響が予想できないんです（笑）。これは公式なものではありませんよね。公式ではなく、極秘インタビューでもないですよね。

石川　これは公式な声明ではありませんが、あなたの真意や、ほんとうの考えが明らかになるものです。

キャロライン守護霊　いえ、いえ。真意は「推測」しかできませんよ。

石川　分かりました。始めてもよろしいでしょうか。

キャロライン守護霊　結構ですよ。

日本の現状は「問題ない」
石川　あなたは暗殺されたＪ・Ｆ・ケネディ大統領の、現在生きている唯一のお子さんであると思います。

キャロライン守護霊　"お子さん！"

1 Caroline's Guardian Spirit Makes an "Informal" Appearance

Ishikawa Yes, the only living child.

Caroline's G.S. 56-year-old child! (laughs)

Ishikawa Because your father is very famous...

Caroline's G.S. OK, OK. No problem.

Ishikawa I think your appointment to this post shows that President Obama places strong importance on Japan-U.S. ties. We, Japanese people are very happy, and I think you also received a warm welcome from Japanese people.

石川　はい、唯一、生きているお子さんですよね。

キャロライン守護霊　56歳の「お子さん」ですか！（笑）

石川　あなたのお父様はとても有名なので……。

キャロライン守護霊　大丈夫、大丈夫。問題ありません。

石川　あなたがこの地位に任命されたのは、オバマ大統領が日米の結びつきを非常に重視していることの表れであると思います。私たち日本人は大変喜んでいますし、あなたも日本の人たちから温かい歓迎を受けたことと思います。

John F. Kennedy (1917-1963)
35th President of the United States of America. (Political spiritual messages entitled "Interview with Kennedy" were given on August 17, 2010, only available in Japanese.)

ジョン・F・ケネディ（1917‐1963）
第35代アメリカ合衆国大統領。（2010年8月17日収録の政治霊言に「ケネディの政治霊言」がある）

1 Caroline's Guardian Spirit Makes an "Informal" Appearance

Caroline's G.S. Thank you, thank you.

Ishikawa Firstly, I would like to ask you about your overall impression of Japan. I think you came to Japan last November. More than two months have passed.

Caroline's G.S. You, Japanese, already praised us. I came here just to play or for the purpose of leisure (laughs).

Ishikawa No, no. You are expected to help strengthen our ties.

1 キャロライン守護霊「非公式に」登場

キャロライン守護霊　ありがとう、ありがとう。

石川　まず初めに、日本についての全般的(ぜんぱんてき)な印象についてお尋(たず)ねしたいと思います。昨年の11月に日本にいらしたんですよね。もう2ヵ月以上経ったわけですが。

キャロライン守護霊　日本の皆(みな)さんは、すでに私どものことをほめたたえてくださっていますので。私は遊びに来たというか、余暇(よか)を楽しみに来ただけなんです（笑）。

石川　いえいえ、あなたは日米の絆(きずな)を強めることを期待されています。

A horse-drawn carriage carrying the new U.S. Ambassador to Japan Caroline Kennedy. Spectators welcome her as she heads toward the Imperial Palace in Tokyo to meet Japan's Emperor Akihito in a ceremonial formality. (November 19, 2013)

信任状奉呈式のため皇居に向かうキャロライン・ケネディ新駐日大使を載せた馬車と、沿道で歓迎する人々（2013年11月19日）。

1 Caroline's Guardian Spirit Makes an "Informal" Appearance

Caroline's G.S. Expected?

Ishikawa Yes. Because the current situation is very difficult.

Caroline's G.S. Oh, really? Is it difficult?

Ishikawa Yes.

Caroline's G.S. I don't think so. It's very easy.

Ishikawa I think you are expected to deal with…

Caroline's G.S. You are a great country. Japanese people are great. So, there's no problem.

Ishikawa Things such as the chilly Japan–China and Japan–South Korea relations, and the TPP★…

*Trans-Pacific Strategic Economic Partnership Agreement [TPP]. A multi-national free trade agreement between transpacific countries.

1　キャロライン守護霊「非公式に」登場

キャロライン守護霊　期待ですか。

石川　そうです。今は、非常に厳しい状況ですので。

キャロライン守護霊　まあ、ほんとうに？　厳しいんですか。

石川　はい。

キャロライン守護霊　私はそう思いませんね。非常に簡単ですよ。

石川　あなたが期待されているのは……。

キャロライン守護霊　日本は立派な国です。日本人は立派です。ですから、問題はありません。

石川　日中や日韓の冷え切った関係に対処することや、ＴＰＰ（注）など……。

（注）環太平洋パートナーシップ協定。環太平洋地域の国々による経済の自由化を目的とした多角的な経済連携協定。

Caroline's G.S. No problem. Here is Happy Science. No problem (laughs).

Ishikawa Could you answer my question?

Caroline's G.S. I already answered your question.

Ishikawa Your overall impression of Japan.

Caroline's G.S. I am an ambassador, so I need diplomacy.

Ishikawa You are the first female ambassador to Japan.

Caroline's G.S. The first female ambassador. Hmm.

Ishikawa It is a historical appointment.

Caroline's G.S. Hmm. Mr. Obama thought that I would be a good ambassador to Japan because Japanese

1　キャロライン守護霊「非公式に」登場

キャロライン守護霊　問題ありません。ここには幸福の科学があります。問題ありません（笑）。

石川　質問にお答えいただけますでしょうか。

キャロライン守護霊　すでにご質問にはお答えしましたよ。

石川　日本の全般的な印象についてです。

キャロライン守護霊　私は大使ですから、外交術が必要なんです。

石川　あなたは初の女性駐日大使ですよね。

キャロライン守護霊　初の女性大使。うーん。

石川　歴史的な任命です。

キャロライン守護霊　うーん。オバマさんは、日本人はだいたいにおいてケネディ大統領が好きだから、私がい

people usually like President Kennedy. Japanese people think that they were thought much of because of this appointment as an ambassador, as I'm the daughter of President Kennedy. Japanese people think highly of this matter.

Ishikawa You are still very perfect. (Holds up the recent book on JFK) I think this is your latest book, right?

Caroline's G.S. Am I beautiful? OK, OK, OK.

Ishikawa I think you were also involved in publishing this book. This book was also translated into Japanese, so many Japanese people expect from you in your work.

Caroline's G.S. Hundreds of Japanese people might read that book (laughs).

い大使になれると思ったんでしょうね。私はケネディ大統領の娘ですので、私が駐日大使に任命されたことで、日本の人たちは、重視されているように思いますよね。日本人は、そのことを高く評価してくれています。

石川　あなただって大変立派な方です。（Ｊ・Ｆ・ケネディに関する最近の本を示して）これはあなたの最新の本ですよね。

キャロライン守護霊　私は綺麗に写っていますか。ああ、いいですね。

石川　この本の出版にも携わっていらっしゃったと思います。この本は日本語にも翻訳されています。ですから、多くの日本人があなたのお仕事に期待しています。

キャロライン守護霊　読んでくださる日本人が、何百人かは、いるかもしれませんね（笑）。

2 Her View on Japan-U.S. and Japan-China Relations

Wada Hello, Ms. Kennedy. I would like to ask about the relationship between the U.S. and Japan.

Caroline's G.S. The relationship between the U.S. and Japan?

Wada You mentioned in your speech at the Senate Foreign Relations Committee that Japan is an indispensable partner in the issues of trade, security and humanitarian efforts. So how exactly do you plan to strengthen the ties between the U.S. and Japan?

Caroline's G.S. You speak like an American. Oh, I'm happy. Incredible!

Ishikawa She was born in Massachusetts.

2　日米・日中関係をどう見るか

和田　ケネディさん、こんにちは。私からは米日関係についてお伺いしたいと思います。

キャロライン守護霊　米日関係ですか。

和田　あなたは上院の外交委員会でのスピーチで、「日本は、貿易、安全保障、人道的努力の面で不可欠のパートナーである」とおっしゃいました。具体的には、どのようにして米国と日本の絆を強めようと思っていらっしゃいますか。

キャロライン守護霊　あなたの話し方はアメリカ人みたいですね。うれしいわ。信じられない！

石川　彼女はマサチューセッツ州生まれですので。

2 Her View on Japan-U.S. and Japan-China Relations

Caroline's G.S. I know. That's the reason. Her English is not Japanese-like. I've never heard such kind of English in Japan.

Ishikawa She actually graduated from an American university.

Caroline's G.S. Really? I got it.

Ishikawa Born and raised in America.

Caroline's G.S. You are an ambassador, too?

Wada I aspire to be a bridge between the U.S. and Japan. So it is a great honor to be able to speak to you.

Caroline's G.S. OK, OK. What was the question?

Wada So, how do you plan to strengthen the ties between Japan and the U.S.?

キャロライン守護霊　ああ、それでなんですね。彼女の英語は日本人っぽくないですね。日本で、こんな英語は聞いたことがありません。

石川　彼女は実は、アメリカの大学を卒業しているんです。

キャロライン守護霊　ほんとうですか？　なるほど。

石川　生まれも育ちもアメリカです。

キャロライン守護霊　あなたも大使なんですか。

和田　私は「米国と日本の架け橋」になることを志しています。ですから、あなたとお話ができて、大変、光栄です。

キャロライン守護霊　OK、OK。質問は何でしたっけ。

和田　どのようにして日米の絆を強めようとお考えですか。

2 Her View on Japan-U.S. and Japan-China Relations

Caroline's G.S. It's a formal question.

Ishikawa Yes.

Caroline's G.S. You can answer the question yourselves. I am the ambassador, so you can guess and think of an answer to that question. I just want to tighten the ties between the two countries, of course, formally. This is my mission from President Obama.

Ishikawa OK.

Caroline's G.S. I cannot make my heart clear because I must learn diplomacy.

Air Defense Identification Zone over East China Sea
Ishikawa I would like to ask a question from a different angle. Last November, China established their

キャロライン守護霊　フォーマルな質問ですね。

石川　はい。

キャロライン守護霊　ご自分たちで答えてくださって結構ですよ。私は大使ですから、あなたがたがその質問の答えを推測して考えていただいて結構です。公式には、私はもちろん二国間の絆を強めたいと思っています。それがオバマ大統領から与(あた)えられた使命ですから。

石川　分かりました。

キャロライン守護霊　本心を明かすわけにはいきません。外交術を身につけないといけませんので。

東シナ海の防空識別権について

石川　別の角度からお尋ねします。昨年11月、中国は東シナ海上に「防空識別圏(ぼうくうしきべつけん)」（次ページ注）を設定しました。

Air Defense Identification Zone (ADIZ)* over East China Sea. The area includes Senkaku Islands, which are now controlled by Japan.

Caroline's G.S. Uh huh. It is controlled by Japan now?

Ishikawa Yes, right now.

Caroline's G.S. It is, now?

Ishikawa Yes, now.

Caroline's G.S. Controlled by Japan?

Ishikawa Yes.

Caroline's G.S. Now? Is?

---

*The area which extends beyond a country's airspace, that is required in the interest of national security. The zone is constantly under surveillance. An aircraft which does not notify the country of ADIZ prior to flight, but which enters the zone, must identify and prove itself. Military action may be taken to prevent the intrusion of possibly hostile aircraft.

2　日米・日中関係をどう見るか

この中には尖閣諸島も含まれています。尖閣は現在、日本の支配下にあります。

キャロライン守護霊　ああ。現在は日本が支配しているんですか。

石川　はい、今現在は。

キャロライン守護霊　現在「している」んですね。

石川　はい、現在は。

キャロライン守護霊　日本によって支配されている？

石川　はい。

キャロライン守護霊　現在？　されている？

（注）国防上の必要性から、各国が領空とは別に定めた空域のこと。常に監視を行い、あらかじめ飛行計画を提出せずここに進入する航空機に識別と証明を求め、領空侵犯の可能性がある航空機に対しては、軍事的予防措置などを行使することもある。

Ishikawa What do you mean?

Caroline's G.S. It means there's no problem.

Ishikawa Are you serious?

(Audience laughs)

Caroline's G.S. (Laughs) If you were intruded by them, it's a problem. But if you are controlling the islands, it's no problem.

Ishikawa But in your statement, you said that this announcement (by China) undermines security and constitutes an attempt to change the status quo in the East China Sea, and this only serves to increase tensions in the region and create unnecessary risk. This is your official statement...

Caroline's G.S. OK. Someone wrote that statement.

石川　何をおっしゃりたいのでしょうか。

キャロライン守護霊　であれば、問題ありませんね。

石川　本気でおっしゃってるんですか。

（会場笑）

キャロライン守護霊　（笑）もし彼らに侵略されたなら問題です。でも、日本が支配しているなら、問題ありません。

石川　しかし、あなたは声明の中で「（中国による）この発表は、安全を脅かし、東シナ海の現体制を変更する試みとなるでしょう。これは、かの地域の緊張を高め、不必要なリスクを生むことにしかなりません」とおっしゃいました。これは正式な声明ですが……。

キャロライン守護霊　はい。誰かが書いた声明ですよ。

2 Her View on Japan-U.S. and Japan-China Relations

Yes (laughs).

Ishikawa This is not your statement?

Caroline's G.S. Someone wrote it, and I read it. I read the statement.

Ishikawa Secretary of State John Kerry wrote it? Or…?

Caroline's G.S. John Kerry is a poor writer, so he did not. Someone else.

Ishikawa Additionally, Obama's administration told commercial airlines that they must abide by Beijing's call to notify any plans to traverse the newly declared zone over East China Sea. This stance is not in accordance to that of the Japanese government. This is also calling for controversies. Do you have any opinion on this?

そう(笑)。

石川　あなたの声明ではないのですか。

キャロライン守護霊　誰かが書いて、その声明を私が読んだだけです。

石川　それを書いたのは、ジョン・ケリー国務長官ですか。あるいは……。

キャロライン守護霊　ジョン・ケリーは文章を書くのは得意ではないので、書いていません。ほかの誰かです。

石川　さらに、オバマ政権は民間航空会社に対し、「東シナ海上に新たに設定された識別圏を通過する場合はいかなる際も計画を事前通告せよ」という北京政府の要求に従わなければならないと伝えました。この立場は、日本政府の立場とは一致していません。これも議論の余地があります。これについて何かご意見はありますか。

2 Her View on Japan-U.S. and Japan-China Relations

Caroline's G.S. We must prevent unfortunate accidents between China and the United States. So we must let them know our flight plans beforehand to protect our... you said, commercial airlines?

Ishikawa Yes. Japanese commercial airlines are not submitting their flight plans as instructed by their government.

Caroline's G.S. It's our obligation to protect them. Just give one word, "Our flight is at *naninani* (blah-blah) o'clock" and just notify them. We can save the lives of the United States citizens.

But it's your option if you want to let them know the plan or not. If you have enough confidence in your self-defense attitude, you can decide whether to let them know your flight plans or not. And it might be... if there occurred some accident, your government would be accused of the fact. If any Japanese life was to be lost at that time, your government must take some responsibility regarding that.

キャロライン守護霊 中国と米国の間で不幸な事故が起きないようにしないといけません。ですから、私たちの「民間航空会社」——そう言われましたでしょうか——を守るためには、事前に飛行計画を彼らに知らせないといけません。

石川　はい、民間航空会社です。政府の指示で、日本の民間航空会社は飛行計画を提出していません。

キャロライン守護霊 彼らを守るのは私たちの義務です。一言だけ言えばいいでしょう。「われわれのフライトは〇〇時(ナニナニ)である」とだけ伝えておけば、米国民の命を守ることができるんです。

　けれども、日本が計画を伝えたいかどうかは、あなたがたの選択(せんたく)です。もし自分たちの自衛力に十分自信があるなら、飛行計画を知らせるかどうか、自分たちで決めることができます。たぶん……もし何らかの事故が起きたら、日本政府はその事実に関して非難されるでしょう。もし、そのとき日本人の命が失われたら、政府がそれに関して何らかの責任を負わなければなりません。

2 Her View on Japan-U.S. and Japan-China Relations

We must be careful on containing China

Ishikawa Former Secretary of State Hillary Clinton tried to contain China with Japan and South Korea.

Caroline's G.S. Yes, yes.

Ishikawa What do you think about her diplomatic policy?

Caroline's G.S. It's a hot matter. Hillary Clinton is a frontrunner of the next presidential election, so I must be careful about that. She's nice, clever and… that's all (laughs).

Hillary Rodham Clinton (1947-) Served as a senator (Democratic Party) from January 2001 to January 2009, and as the Secretary of State from 2009 to 2013 under the Obama administration. Wife of Bill Clinton, the 42nd President of the United States of America.

ヒラリー・R・クリントン（1947－）2001年1月～2009年1月まで上院議員（民主党）、2009年から2013年までオバマ政権で国務長官を務める。第42代大統領ビル・クリントン夫人。

2 日米・日中関係をどう見るか

中国封じ込め戦略には慎重

石川　ヒラリー・クリントン前米国務長官は、日本や韓国と一緒に中国を封じ込めようとしました。

キャロライン守護霊　はい、はい。

石川　彼女の外交政策に関してはどう思われますか。

キャロライン守護霊　それはホットな問題ですね。ヒラリー・クリントンは、次の大統領選に向けたトップランナーですから、私もその点には気をつけないと。彼女はいい人で、聡明で……以上です（笑）。

Spiritual Reading on Hillary Clinton: Politics and Foreign Diplomacy (2012, Tentative title)
The guardian spirit of Mrs. Clinton spoke about her vigiliance on China's expansionism.

『ヒラリー・クリントンの政治外交リーディング』
（2012年 幸福実現党刊）
クリントン氏の守護霊は中国の拡張主義に対する警戒感などを語った。

2 Her View on Japan-U.S. and Japan-China Relations

Ishikawa Do you support her diplomatic policy? Yes or no?

Caroline's G.S. Containing China is a little difficult, I guess.

Ishikawa Then officially, do you support her policy?

Caroline's G.S. Officially…

Ishikawa But in your mind? Is it neutral? Does it depend on the situation?

Caroline's G.S. She is planning to be the next president of the United States. The first female president of the United States. So I should obey her opinion. So, yes.

Ishikawa Maybe presidency is the final glass ceiling for American women.

石川　彼女の外交政策を支持されますか。「イエス」か「ノー」で。

キャロライン守護霊　中国を封じ込めるのは、ちょっと難しいのではないかと思います。

石川　では、公式には、あなたは彼女の政策を支持されますか。

キャロライン守護霊　公式にはね……。

石川　でも本心は？　中立ですか。場合によりますか。

キャロライン守護霊　彼女は次の合衆国大統領になろうと思って計画中です。合衆国で初めての女性大統領です。なので、彼女の意見には従うべきでしょうね。ですから、イエスです。

石川　大統領の地位は、アメリカの女性に残された最後の見えない壁かもしれませんね。

Caroline's G.S. So it may be possible to contain China regarding the Senkaku Islands matter only. Not all over China because we, the United States, have a lot of foreign trade with China. China has a lot of bucks, I mean U.S. dollars, and treasury bonds. So we must be careful regarding economic matters.

3 True Emotions Behind America's Disappointment in Yasukuni Visit

Ishikawa I think you are very close to President Obama. I think you strongly supported Obama in both 2008 and 2012 presidential elections. You enjoy

キャロライン守護霊　尖閣問題に限ってなら、中国を封じ込めることは可能かもしれません。中国全体ではなく。米国は中国と多額の貿易を行っていますし、中国は米ドルや米国債（べいこくさい）をたくさん持っていますので。ですから経済問題については注意しないといけません。

3　米国が靖国参拝に「失望」の真意は

石川　あなたはオバマ大統領と非常に近い関係にあると思います。2008年と2012年の二度の大統領選挙戦でも、オバマを強く支持されたと思います。あなたは彼とは親

President Obama and Caroline Kennedy at the presidential campaign in Scranton, Pennsylvania, on April 20, 2008.

2008年4月20日、大統領選キャンペーンでのオバマ大統領とキャロライン・ケネディ（ペンシルバニア州スクラントン市にて）。

such a close relationship with him, that you have direct telephone access to him. How do you feel about President Obama's stance? Is it the same as Hillary Clinton, or is it different?

Caroline's G.S. No, it's a little different. Mrs. Clinton is a hard negotiator, but Mr. Obama is not. He prefers "soft landing," so it's a little different.

Ishikawa Vice President Joe Biden tried to persuade Prime Minister Abe not to visit Yasukuni Shrine, because it is very controversial.

3　米国が靖国参拝に「失望」の真意は

しい関係にあるので、直接電話もされる間柄です。オバマ大統領のスタンスについては、どうお感じですか。ヒラリー・クリントンと同じですか。それとも違いますか。

キャロライン守護霊　はい、少し違います。クリントンさんはハード・ネゴシエーター（手ごわい交渉相手）ですけれども、オバマさんは違いますね。彼はソフト・ランディング（軟着陸）のほうが好きなので、少し違います。

石川　ジョー・バイデン副大統領が、安倍首相に靖国神社へ参拝しないよう説得を試みました。非常に論議を巻き起こすからと。

Yasukuni Shrine
Roughly 2.5 million nation-devoted souls since the end of Edo Era are worshipped.

靖国神社。江戸幕末以降の戦死者など、約250万人が祀られている。

Caroline's G.S. Prime Minister Abe? Not to visit Yasukuni Shrine? Ah, it's a crucial point and a very difficult point. It's related to my... (taps neck many times) you know?

Ishikawa As you know, convicted war criminals are commemorated in the shrine.

Caroline's G.S. Yes, I know, I know.

Wada In America, there's the Arlington National Cemetery of Virginia, where war heroes who fought for the country are buried. And although there are

3　米国が靖国参拝に「失望」の真意は

キャロライン守護霊　安倍首相に？　靖国神社へ参拝しないように？　ああ、きわめて重要で難しい問題です。私の（首筋を手で何度も叩きながら）……が、かかっています。お分かりですか。

石川　ご存じのように、あの神社には戦犯として有罪になった人たちが祀られています。

キャロライン守護霊　はい、知っています。分かります。

和田　アメリカには、バージニア州にアーリントン国立墓地があって、国のために戦った英霊が埋葬されています。南軍の兵士たちも埋葬されていますが、多くの人が

Arlington National Cemetery
A U.S. military cemetery located in Virginia. Former President Kennedy is also buried here.

アーリントン国立墓地
バージニア州にあるアメリカ合衆国の戦没者慰霊施設。ケネディ大統領もここに埋葬されている。

even Confederate soldiers there, many people go there to pay tribute. Don't you think it is the same thing in Yasukuni Shrine, where we…

Caroline's G.S. No, no, no.

Wada give our respect to…

Caroline's G.S. No, no, no. Officially, no. Partly yes, but officially, no.

Wada What is your opinion?

Caroline's G.S. My opinion is, it's up to Japan. Japanese people should choose their future. We, America, cannot stop you from visiting Yasukuni Shrine because of Japanese religious thoughts. You, Japanese also must have the freedom of religion. You can choose religious activities. It's too much if we argue so much on whether you visiting your shrine is good

訪れて敬意を捧げています。靖国神社も同じことだと思われませんか。靖国でも……。

キャロライン守護霊　いいえ、違います、違います。

和田　私たちは尊敬の……

キャロライン守護霊　いいえ、違います、違います。公式には違います。部分的にはイエスですが、公式には違います。

和田　あなたのご意見は、いかがですか。

キャロライン守護霊　私の意見では、その点は日本次第です。日本の皆さんが自分の未来を選ぶべきです。日本の宗教的な考え方がありますので、私たちアメリカは、あなたがたの靖国神社参拝をとめることはできません。日本の皆さんにも信教の自由がなければいけませんし、宗教的行為を選ぶことができるわけですから、靖国神社に参拝することがいいかどうかについて、私たちがあまり議論するのは、

or not. We would be intruding on your rights, opinion and your style of traditional life.

Ishikawa However, in December, the United States Embassy in Japan said in their statement that the United States is disappointed that the Japanese leader had taken an action.

Caroline's G.S. Disappointed is OK. It's just on our side. The American side. The people of the United States or the representatives of the people of the United States can be disappointed. It's our matter. But…

Ishikawa I have another question. I think you were in Kyoto at the moment this statement was made public.

Caroline's G.S. Someone wrote it.

Ishikawa Is this a serious statement from you?

行き過ぎです。あなたがたの権利や意見や伝統的な生活習慣を侵害(しんがい)することになってしまいます。

石川　しかし、12月に日本の米大使館は声明の中で「日本の指導者が行動を取ったことに米国は失望している」と言いました。

キャロライン守護霊　「失望」は構わないんです。私たちの側のことですから。アメリカ側のことです。米国民や米国民の代表は、失望してもいいんです。私たちの問題です。けれども……。

石川　もう一つ質問です。この声明が出されたとき、あなたは京都にいらっしゃったと思いますが。

キャロライン守護霊　誰かが書いたんですよ。

石川　この声明は、あなたの本心からのものですか。

Caroline's G.S. Umm. Here in Japan, people should not speak straightly. Sometimes we must say different things from which we are holding in our mind. Japanese conversation is very difficult. You don't rely on the words of other people. You just rely on your non-verbal communication. *Haragei* communication is a very important thing. Verbal communication is not so important in Japan. Sometimes verbal communication is misleading in Japan. We said that we were disappointed. It just means disappointed. It just means we don't support attacking the Chinese attitude. That's all.

Her stance towards Japan-South Korea issues

Ishikawa OK. I think you recently met with the Korean Ambassador to Japan.

Caroline's G.S. Korean Ambassador in Japan… Difficult questions! No, no, no, no. OK.

キャロライン守護霊　うーん。ここ日本ではストレートに物を言ってはいけないんです。心の中で思っているのとは違うことを言わなければならないこともあるわけです。日本語の会話は非常に難しいんです。他人の言葉を頼（たよ）りにするのではなく、非言語的コミュニケーションにこそ頼るわけです。「腹芸（はらげい）」が非常に大事なんです。日本では言語的コミュニケーションは、さほど重要ではありません。日本では言語的コミュニケーションは誤解を招くこともあります。私たちは「失望している」と言いましたが、それは単に「失望している」というだけの意味です。「中国の姿勢を攻撃（こうげき）することは支持しない」という意味であって、それだけのことですよ。

日韓問題に対するスタンス

石川　分かりました。あなたは最近、駐日韓国大使と会われたと思います。

キャロライン守護霊　駐日韓国大使……難しい質問ばかり！　ノー、ノー、ノー、ノー。分かりました。

Ishikawa I think South Korean Ambassador Lee must have spoken of the importance for Japan to own up to 1993's statement by then-Chief Cabinet Secretary Yohei Kono,* which acknowledged Japanese military responsibility for the forced recruitment of women into sexual servitude during the war.

Caroline's G.S. Ahh.

Ishikawa But it remains unknown. How did you respond? This is not revealed.

*The Kono Statement: A discourse on comfort women that was issued by then-Chief Cabinet Secretary Yohei Kono under the Miyazawa administration in 1993. This discourse stated that, during World War II, the Japanese Imperial Army "was directly or perhaps indirectly involved" in setting up and managing comfort stations, as well as in transferring comfort women. The discourse also says, therefore, that Japan expresses "deep apology and a heart of repentance." However, a Cabinet decision has not been made on this. Upon further investigations, it bacame clear that this discourse was based on groundless rumors that have not been proven with any historical facts. Therefore, opinions are being raised to review the discourse.

石川　韓国の李大使は、1993年当時の河野洋平内閣官房長官による談話（注）に関し、日本が責任をとることの重要性を話したはずだと思います。戦争中に日本軍が、女性を強制的に性的奴隷として集めたことの責任を認めた談話です。

キャロライン守護霊　ああ。

石川　しかし、会話の内容は知られていません。あなたはどう答えたのでしょうか。公表されていませんので。

Reprehending Kono Statement and Murayama Statement (2013, Tentative title)
　In this book, the guardian spirits of former Chief Cabinet Secretary Kono and former Prime Minister Tomiichi Murayama confessed that their statements were not based on historical fact.

『「河野談話」「村山談話」を斬る！』（2013年 幸福の科学出版）
　本書で河野前官房長官と村山富市元首相らの守護霊は、自らの談話が歴史的事実に基づいていないことを告白した。

（注）河野談話：1993年に、宮沢内閣の河野洋平官房長官が発表した慰安婦関係調査結果発表のこと。第2次世界大戦中、朝鮮半島での慰安所の設置や管理、慰安婦の移送について旧日本軍が「直接あるいは間接に関与した」とし、元慰安婦に対して「心からお詫びと反省の気持ち」を表明した。しかし、これは、政府による閣議決定はされていない。その後の検証により、歴史的事実として証拠のない風評を公式見解としたものであることが明らかになり、見直しの声が上がっている。

Caroline's G.S. Difficult question. Again, I cannot answer.

Ishikawa Because you are known as a human rights advocate.

Caroline's G.S. It depends on the historical fact. If South Korea's saying is correct and you were bad several decades ago, then they are in the right situation. But if the saying is faulty or false, you were right and you should say something to them. You must protect the honor of your ancestors. I think so. It depends on

3　米国が靖国参拝に「失望」の真意は

キャロライン守護霊　難しい質問で、また、お答えできません。

石川　あなたは人権擁護派(じんけんようごは)として知られていますので。

キャロライン守護霊　それは歴史的事実によります。もし韓国の言い分が正しくて、あなたがたが数十年前に悪いことをしたのであれば、彼らの立場は正当です。けれども、もし彼らの言い分が誤りないし偽(いつわ)りであるとしたら、あなたがたが正しかったのであり、何らかのことを言うべきです。先祖の名誉(めいよ)を守らなければなりません。そう思います。真実の歴

(Left) *The Truth on the Comfort Women Problem and Nanking Massacre* (2012, Tentative title)
(左)『従軍慰安婦問題と南京大虐殺は本当か？』（2012年 幸福の科学出版刊）

(Middle) *Can You Swear to God that "Comfort Women" Really Existed?* (2013, Tentative title)
(中)『神に誓って「従軍慰安婦」は実在したか』（2013年 幸福実現党刊）

(Right) *South Korea's Conspiracy* (2013, IRH Press Co., Ltd.)
(右)『安重根は韓国の英雄か、それとも悪魔か』（2013年 幸福の科学出版刊）

From the spiritual messages of these three books, it became apparent that the allegation of comfort women by South Korea was not a historical fact.

三冊の霊言によって、従軍慰安婦に関する韓国側の言い分は歴史的真実ではないことが明らかになっている。

the real historical fact. But I'm not a professional of such kind, so I can say nothing about that. This is the standing point of diplomacy. You know (laughs)?

Ishikawa For example, last year, U.N. Secretary General Ban Ki-moon said that Japan needs to have a correct historical view.

Caroline's G.S. It's bad, it's bad. He should not say such a thing.

Ishikawa Right, right.

Caroline's G.S. He must be neutral. He must

史的事実によります。ただ、私はその道のプロではありませんので、その点については何も申し上げられません。これが外交的立場というものです。お分かりですね？（笑）

石川　たとえば昨年、国連の潘基文(バン キ ムン)事務総長は、「日本は〝正しい歴史認識〟を持つ必要がある」と言いました。

キャロライン守護霊　それはだめです、だめです。そんなことを言うべきではありません。

石川　はい、はい。

キャロライン守護霊　彼は中立でなければいけません。

Unmasking Ban Ki-Moon's Biased Stance (2013, IRH Press Co., Ltd.)
In this book, it was revealed that Mr. Ban's subconscious thinks only of the profits of South Korea.

『潘基文国連事務総長の守護霊インタビュー』（2013年 幸福の科学出版刊）
潘氏の潜在意識は韓国の利益しか考えていないことが本書で明かされた。

abandon his role as a foreign minister of South Korea. He used to be a South Korean foreign minister, but he should abandon that standing point and must be on neutral position of the United Nations.

Wada It seemed like you did not have a clear vision or clear stance of what you wish to do as the ambassador to Japan. Could you tell us more of what you wish to accomplish as ambassador?

Caroline's G.S. I was told that I came here to enjoy Japanese stay.

Ishikawa (Laughs) Is that your mission?

Caroline's G.S. My mission is to enjoy the stay in Japan and be a good friend to Japanese people. That's all. So there is no decision required. I am not a decision-maker. Decision must be made in the United States. So…

韓国の外務大臣としての役割は捨てなければいけません。彼はかつて韓国の外務大臣でしたが、そういう立場は捨てて、国連の中立な立場に立たなければいけません。

和田　あなたは駐日大使として何がしたいのか、明確なビジョンやスタンスをお持ちでなかったように見えるのですが、大使として何を成し遂げたいのか、もっとお聞かせいただけますでしょうか。

キャロライン守護霊　私は、「日本滞在を楽しむため」と言われて来ていますので。

石川　（笑）それが、あなたの使命なんですか。

キャロライン守護霊　私の使命は、「日本滞在を楽しんで、日本の人たちと良き友人になること」です。それだけなんです。判断は求められていません。私は意思決定者ではありません。意思決定は米国でなされないといけませんので……。

4 World War II

Ishikawa I think you first visited Hiroshima in 1978, with your uncle, Senator Edward Kennedy.

Caroline's G.S. Yes. Yes, yes, yes.

Ishikawa And I heard you were very moved by that visit. I think you are…

Caroline's G.S. You… (shows discomfort)

Ishikawa This is a historical fact.

Caroline's G.S. You bad guy. Bad guy! Your intention is very evil!

Ishikawa And your great father, President Kennedy, was very proud that he was able to start the process of

4　第二次世界大戦をどう考えるか

石川　あなたは1978年に初めて広島に行かれたと思います。あなたの叔父上であるエドワード・ケネディ上院議員と一緒に。

キャロライン守護霊　はい。はい、はい、はい。

石川　そして、その訪問で非常に心を動かされたとお聞きしました。たぶん、あなたは……。

キャロライン守護霊　あなたは……（嫌な表情をする）。

石川　これは歴史的事実ですので。

キャロライン守護霊　嫌な人ですね。嫌な人！　あなたの狙いには、非常に悪意を感じますよ！

石川　そして、あなたの偉大なお父様であるケネディ大統領は、核軍縮のプロセスを始めることができたのを、

nuclear disarmament, right? After the Cuban Missile Crisis, your father started negotiating with the Soviet Union and the U.K. regarding the Limited Test Ban Treaty. I think you also visited Nagasaki in December.

Caroline's G.S. Nagasaki, yes.

Ishikawa And additionally, Obama gave a speech in Prague.

Caroline's G.S. Yes, yes.

Ishikawa Yes, yes. "As a nuclear power, as the only nuclear power to have used a nuclear weapon, the United States has a moral responsibility to act." And, "I state clearly and with conviction, America's commitment to seek the peace and security of a world without nuclear weapons." And, many survivors and activists have repeatedly called for an American president to visit the cities, Nagasaki and Hiroshima.

非常に誇りに思っておられましたよね。キューバのミサイル危機のあと、お父様は部分的核実験禁止条約に関してソ連やイギリスと交渉を開始されました。あなたは12月に長崎にも行かれたと思いますが。

キャロライン守護霊　長崎ね、はい。

石川　また、オバマは、プラハで演説しました。

キャロライン守護霊　はい、はい。

石川　はい、そうです。「核保有国として、核兵器を使用したことがある唯一の核保有国として、米国は行動する道義的な責任を持っています」と。そして、「私は明白に、確信を持って、アメリカが核兵器のない平和で安全な世界を追求することを約束します」と。また、多くの生存者や活動家が、アメリカの大統領に、長崎や広島を訪問するよう繰り返し求めています。オバマ大統領に、広島や長崎を訪問するよう説得することが、あなたにとって

I think this is a very important mission for you to persuade President Obama to visit Hiroshima and Nagasaki. Are you going to do that?

Caroline's G.S. Hmm, ahh. You are a hard negotiator.

Ishikawa Ah, sorry.

Caroline's G.S. Ah, I'm pleasured that you do not come from Korea or China. You are Japanese, so you should not insist that point repeatedly.

Obama wants to visit Hiroshima and Nagasaki

Caroline's G.S. Ahh, ahh. Mr. Obama sincerely thinks that he'd like to go to Hiroshima and Nagasaki, and wants to appeal his real hope of world peace. It might be real, but he's the president now, so it's a very difficult problem. That kind of nuclear weapon

非常に重要な使命なのではないかと思います。そうするつもりはありますか。

キャロライン守護霊　うーん、ああ。あなたは手ごわい交渉人ですね。

石川　ああ、申し訳ありません。

キャロライン守護霊　ああ、あなたが韓国や中国の出身でなくて、よかったですよ。あなたは日本人ですから、その点は何度も主張しないようにしてください。

オバマは広島・長崎を訪れたい

キャロライン守護霊　ああ、ああ。オバマさんは、広島や長崎に行って、自分が本心から願っている世界平和を訴えたいと、本気で思ってますよ。それは本当かもしれません。けれども、彼は今、大統領ですから、それはとても難しい問題なんです。そんな（広島、長崎で使われたような）核

(dropped on Hiroshima and Nagasaki) is also protecting Japan now, because you are projected to the attack from North Korea, China and other countries. Hmm.

So we must save Japanese people at that time. It is easy for Mr. Obama to say that kind of a thing, but he must also keep the promise to protect Japan. That is his dilemma, and I must represent him. In the near future, I'll go to Hiroshima and Nagasaki, and pray for peace instead of Mr. Obama.

But he's planning to come to Japan this April. I don't know exactly what he intends to do. But if he wants to do so, I mean visit Hiroshima and Nagasaki, its political meaning is very difficult to understand and interpret for other people, or how to understand its content. Politicians are very difficult people to understand. Sometimes they are thinking of another objective that is not in accordance with their conduct.

So, Mr. Obama will come soon and say something. He will say something about the peace of Far East Asia.

兵器であっても、今の日本を守っているんです。あなたがたは、北朝鮮や中国や、あるいはその他の国から攻撃対象として想定されているわけですから。うーん。

　ですから、そうなったら、私たちは日本の人たちを救わなければなりません。オバマさんは、そういうことを言うのは簡単ですけれど、「日本を守る」という約束も守らなければいけませんからね。それが彼のジレンマなので、私が彼の代わりにならないといけません。近いうちに広島と長崎に行って、オバマさんの代わりに平和を祈ろうと思います。

　でも、この４月に、彼は日本に来る予定です。何をするつもりか、具体的には知りません。ただ、もし彼がそれを望んでいるとしても、つまり、広島と長崎を訪問したがっているとしても、人々がその政治的意味を理解したり、その内容をどう解釈すべきかを人に説明するのは、非常に難しいことです。政治家というのは非常に理解し難い人たちなんです。行動していることと別のことを考えていることがありますからね。

　ですから、オバマさんは間もなく来て、何か言うでしょう。極東アジアの平和について何らかの発言をするでしょ

He will appeal to Japanese, Korean, South Korean, Chinese and Filipino people, "Be peaceful. Keep your peace in the future. We will be a peacemaker." He will say that he will be a peacemaker. He really wants to become the modern Jesus Christ in his mind. He wants to change from a political personality to a religious personality. It's his final aim, I think.

The spirit of JFK says, "America did too much"

Ishikawa Yes. I think Obama is called *Black Kennedy*.

Caroline's G.S. Oh, *Black Kennedy*!

う。きっと、日本人や朝鮮人、韓国人、中国人、フィリピン人に対して、「平和であってください。将来に向けて平和を保ってください。われわれが仲裁します」と訴えるでしょうね。「自分が仲裁者になる」と言うでしょう。彼は内心、本気で〝現代のイエス・キリスト〟になりたいと思っていますよ。「政治的人間」から「宗教的人間」に変わりたいんです。それが彼の最終目標だと思います。

「アメリカは、やりすぎた」と語ってきた
J・F・ケネディの霊

石川　はい。オバマは「黒人版ケネディ」と呼ばれていると思うのですが。

キャロライン守護霊　おお、「ブラック・ケネディ」！

Have Faith in Great America (2012, IRH Press Co., Ltd.)
In Part II of this book, the real opinions of his subconscious was revealed.

『バラク・オバマのスピリチュアル・メッセージ』　(2012年 幸福実現党刊)
本書でオバマ氏の潜在意識の本音が明かされた。

Ishikawa Yes, yes.

Caroline's G.S. That sounds a little... not so good.

Wada Not so good? What did you think of your father as a person and as a politician?

Caroline's G.S. I was five years old, so my memory is very poor. After I grew up, I read and watched a lot of films about my father. Of course, I have much

石川　はい、はい。

キャロライン守護霊　それはちょっと……あまりいい響きではないですね。

和田　あまりよくないですか。あなたはお父様のことを、一人の人間として、また、一人の政治家として、どう思っていらっしゃったのですか。

キャロライン守護霊　私は5歳でしたから、ほとんど記憶にないんです。大人になってから、父についてたくさん読んだり映像を観たりしました。もちろん、父を深く尊敬し

Mr. and Mrs. Kennedy with young Caroline.
ケネディ夫妻と幼少のキャロライン。

respect for him, but at the time, I had no idea. I was just playing around the White House and usually were laughed at by other people because I was very small and not so, how do I say, well-trained, I mean, a polite child. I was bad at the time.

But I remember the news of my daddy's death. It was very sad and all the people of America were very sad at that time. From the grief of the people, I felt that my father was a very great person and a historical person. At the time, I thought that I must have some responsibility regarding my political future.

ていますけれど、当時は分かりませんでした。私はホワイトハウスの周りで遊んでいただけで、いつも皆から笑われていました。すごく幼かったですし、何と言うか、あまりしつけが良くなくて、つまり礼儀(れいぎ)正しい子ではなかったので。当時は悪い子だったんです。

　でも、パパの死のニュースについては、覚えています。とても悲しかったし、当時、アメリカ人全員がとても悲しみました。人々の悲しみから、父が非常に偉大(いだい)な人で歴史的人物であるのを感じました。自分も将来、政治において何らかの責任を負わなければならないと、その時、思ったんです。

At the funeral of Former President John F. Kennedy, on November 24, 1963. Caroline and her younger brother, John F. Kennedy, Jr., are seen holding hands with Former First Lady Jacqueline Kennedy.

1963年11月25日（日本時間）、ケネディ大統領の葬儀の様子。ジャクリーン夫人に手を引かれるキャロラインと弟のジョン・F・ケネディJr.。

Ishikawa (Holds up the previously mentioned book) In this book's foreword, it says that the generation JFK inspired changed this country; that they fought for civil rights, women's rights, human rights and nuclear disarmament. And I think last year you gave a speech at the Lincoln Memorial. And I think you probably know very well about the shooting of Trayvon Martin. And I think you said, "The Supreme Court eviscerated the Voting Rights Act." Last year, the Supreme Court handed down a not-guilty verdict. So, I have one question.

Caroline's G.S. One question? OK.

Ishikawa About your historical view on World War II, the Pacific War.

Caroline's G.S. Ah-ha!

Ishikawa Yes. Japan…

4　第二次世界大戦をどう考えるか

石川　（先ほどの本を示して）この本のまえがきには、「JFKに鼓舞された世代が、この国を変えた。彼らは、市民権、女性の権利、人権、核武装解除のために戦った」と書かれています。また、あなたは去年、リンカーン記念館でスピーチをされたと思います。そして、たぶんトレイヴォン・マーティンの射殺事件については、よくご存じですよね。そして、あなたは「最高裁判所は投票権法を骨抜きにした」とおっしゃったと思います。去年、最高裁は無罪の判決を言い渡しました。そこで、一つ質問があります。

キャロライン守護霊　一つですね。どうぞ。

石川　歴史観についてです。第二次世界大戦についての。太平洋戦争の。

キャロライン守護霊　ああ！

石川　はい。日本が……。

Caroline's G.S. I got your intention now.

Ishikawa Please do not go away (laughs). Do you think America…

Caroline's G.S. I'm an ambassador, so…

Ishikawa Yes, yes. Do you think America embodied global justice during World War II?

Caroline's G.S. (Sighs)

Ishikawa Roosevelt or Truman?

キャロライン守護霊　やっとあなたの狙いが分かりました。

石川　どうか、お逃げにならないでください（笑）。あなたは、アメリカが……。

キャロライン守護霊　私は大使ですから……。

石川　はい、はい。アメリカは第二次大戦中、地球的正義を体現していたと思われますか。

キャロライン守護霊　（ため息）

石川　ルーズベルトやトルーマンが？

Was the Dropping of the Atomic Bomb a Sin for Humanity? (2013, Tentative title)
『原爆投下は人類への罪か？』（2013年 幸福実現党刊）

4 World War II

Caroline's G.S. (Clicks tongue) Hmm.

Ishikawa After World War II, your father tried to legalize the Civil Rights Act. So maybe American history has some kind of contradictions.

Caroline's G.S. My father just came here and said that his opinion is, "Japan is not so bad. Their honor should be recovered by some political deed. We, Americans, did too much." He said so.*

Ishikawa Thank you so much.

Japanese ancestors were thinking an idealistic future

Caroline's G.S. My opinion might not have so great a weight. I was born after World War II, so I don't

---

*The spirit of J.F. Kennedy apparently told so to Caroline's guardian spirit in the spiritual world.

キャロライン守護霊　（舌打ち）うーん。

石川　第二次大戦後、あなたのお父様は公民権法を制定しようとされました。ですから、アメリカの歴史には何らかの矛盾があるかもしれません。

キャロライン守護霊　父が、たった今ここに来て、言いました。父の意見としては「日本は、さほど悪くない。日本の名誉は、何らかの政治的行為によって回復されねばならない。われわれアメリカ人は、やりすぎた」。そう言いました（注）。

石川　ありがとうございます。

日本の先人たちは理想の未来を考えていた

キャロライン守護霊　私の意見には大して重みがないかもしれません。私は第二次大戦後に生まれたので、第二

（注）霊的世界において、J・F・ケネディの霊がキャロライン守護霊に語ったと思われる。

exactly know the real meaning of World War II. But we are friends now. If we are friends now, we should not have been enemies at the time.

We could have had more compassion and comprehension toward Japan at the time. We could have, but we, American people were just thinking about our profits at that time. Japan got a lot of profits from Asian countries, so we had to stop Japanese military power.

At the time, we thought that Japan was evil, but now we must be more kind to Japanese ancestors. They are not so bad. They were thinking about some kind of idealistic future. I can feel that now.

Ishikawa We also have a political party.

Caroline's G.S. Political party?

次大戦のほんとうの意味は正確には知りません。けれども、私たちは今、友人同士であるわけですから、今友人であるということは、当時、敵同士であってはいけなかったということです。

　私たちは、当時の日本に対して、もっと同情できたはずですし、理解できたはずです。できたはずなのに、私たちアメリカ人は、当時は自分たちの利益のことしか考えていませんでした。日本がアジア諸国から多くの利益を得ていましたので、日本の軍事力を押しとどめなければいけなかったわけです。

　私たちは当時、日本は「悪」であると思っていました。けれども今は、日本の先人たちに対して、もっと心優しくあるべきです。そんなに悪い人たちではないのですから。彼らは、理想の未来のようなものを考えていたんです。今は、そう感じられます。

石川　私たちは政党も持っています。

キャロライン守護霊　政党ですか。

4 World War II

Ishikawa Yes, the Happiness Realization Party. We think that the relationship between Japan and the U.S. is very important. But I think your father said in his inaugural speech, "Let us never negotiate out of fear, but let us never fear to negotiate." So I would like to ask one more question. Commander Douglas MacArthur…

Caroline's G.S. MacArthur!

Ishikawa Yes, yes. After World War II, in 1951 during the Senate Committee, I think he said about the Japanese, "Their purpose, therefore, in going to war

Douglas MacArthur (1880 - 1964)

ダグラス・マッカーサー
（1880 - 1964）

4　第二次世界大戦をどう考えるか

石川　はい、幸福実現党です。私たちは、日米関係が非常に重要だと考えています。しかし、あなたのお父様は就任演説で「恐怖ゆえに交渉してはなりません。しかし、交渉することを恐れてはなりません」とおっしゃったと思います。そこで、もう一つ伺いたいのですが、ダグラス・マッカーサー司令官は……。

キャロライン守護霊　マッカーサーですか！

石川　はい、はい。彼は第二次大戦後、1951年に上院委員会で日本人について、「したがって、彼らが戦争に飛び込んでいった目的は、大部分が安全保障の必要に迫られ

MacArthur's Testimony 65 Years After the War
(2010, Tentative title)
『マッカーサー戦後65年目の証言』
（2010年　幸福の科学出版刊）

MacArthur gives his opinion on post-war Japan from the spiritual world.
霊界に還ったマッカーサーは本書で戦後日本についての見解を述べている。

97

was largely dictated by security." This sentence is well-known to Japanese conservative people. Of course, we can interpret it in a different way. 'Security' has a broad meaning. So, was the Pacific War an war of invasion or a self-defense war? From an American perspective.

Caroline's G.S. OK, but the situation had changed by that time. Douglas MacArthur, General MacArthur, said in the situation of the conflict between communism and capitalism, or the conflict between freedom and totalitarianism. So the situation changed after a period of five years. We, American people had to fight against the North Korean army which was supported by the Chinese army. So at that time, we had to involve Japanese people as an additional war force. We changed our situation, our thinking and opinion at that time. At the time of 1945, our opinion was unchanged. I think so.

てのことだったのです」と言ったと思います。この一文は、日本の保守系の人たちには良く知られています。もちろん、違う解釈もできます。「安全保障」というのは意味が広いですから。そこで、アメリカの視点から見て、太平洋戦争は「侵略戦争」だったのでしょうか、「自衛戦争」だったのでしょうか。

キャロライン守護霊　はい、でも、当時は状況が変わっていたんです。ダグラス・マッカーサーが、つまりマッカーサー元帥がそう言ったのは、「共産主義 対 資本主義」、あるいは「自由 対 全体主義」の争いがある状況の中でした。ですから、その後の５年間で状況が変わったんです。私たちアメリカ人は、中国軍に支えられた北朝鮮軍と戦わなければならなかったので、当時、追加戦力として日本の人たちを巻き込まないといけなかったんです。そのとき、立場や考え方、意見を変えたんです。1945年当時は、意見は変わっていなかったと思います。

5 Comfort Women Issue and Women's Rights

Wada The statue of a comfort woman was built in California and in other cities in America. What do you think about that?

Caroline's G.S. Difficult religion!

(Audience laughs)

Caroline's G.S. Oh... South Korea is also a friendly country. We think that they are our friend, and must protect the army in the northern part of South Korea. So it's very difficult to speak clearly. It's your conflict! Please fight between the two countries. Mr. Abe and Ms. Park should have a Sumo wrestling match. Abe will win. OK.

Saito Can I ask about the situation of women? She

5　慰安婦問題と女性の権利について

和田　慰安婦像が、カリフォルニアやアメリカの他の都市で設置されました。それについては、どう思われますでしょうか。

キャロライン守護霊　難しい宗教ですね！

（会場笑）

キャロライン守護霊　ああ……韓国も友好国ですので。彼らも友人であると思っていますし、韓国北部の軍隊は守らなければいけません。ですから、はっきり言うのは非常に難しいんです。それは、あなたたちの間の争いでしょう！　どうか、二国間で争っていただけますか。安倍さんと朴さんが相撲を取ればいいんです。安倍さんが勝ちますよ。OKです。

斉藤　女性たちが置かれている状況について、伺っても

5 Comfort Women Issue and Women's Rights

asked about comfort women…

Caroline's G.S. Oh, comfort women.

Saito To say such a thing is kind of looking down on women.

Caroline's G.S. Comfort women does not sound good.

Saito No. You're working very hard for women's rights, so how can we, women, promote our status in the world?

Caroline's G.S. Hmm.

Ishikawa I think you met with Prime Minister Abe, and you highly rated his pledge to create a society where women can play more active roles.

よろしいでしょうか。彼女が今、慰安婦について質問しましたが……。

キャロライン守護霊　ああ、慰安婦ですか。

斉藤　そういうことを言うのは、ある意味、女性を見下しています。

キャロライン守護霊　「慰安婦」というのは、いい響きではありませんね。

斉藤　ええ。あなたは、女性の権利に関して非常に熱心に活動されていますが、私たち女性が、世界の女性の地位を上げるためには、どうすればいいでしょうか。

キャロライン守護霊　うーん。

石川　安倍首相とお会いになって、女性がもっと活躍できる社会を作るという安倍首相の決意を大変評価されていたと思います。

5 Comfort Women Issue and Women's Rights

Caroline's G.S. Hmm. Yes. Ahh.

Ishikawa In Japan, unlike America or other countries, there aren't so many women executives. So maybe you want Prime Minister Abe to promote women's status in Japan.

Caroline's G.S. This is true to South Korea, too; these areas... I mean the areas influenced by Confucius, are apt to think that men are superior to women. It's your history and tradition, so it's very difficult to change.

The problem is how you think about the equality of humankind. Our American Constitution says equality of men, and "men" or "man" is a representative of humankind. So historically, we, too, looked down upon females as an inferior existence.

So, the world is changing now. We're very sad about our history regarding black people, I mean the slaves from Africa. And women's rights were very low

5　慰安婦問題と女性の権利について

キャロライン守護霊　うーん、はい。ああ。

石川　日本では、アメリカや他の国々と違って、女性の管理職はあまり多くありません。ですから、たぶん、あなたは安倍首相に、日本の女性の地位を上げてほしいと望んでいるのではありませんか。

キャロライン守護霊　韓国もそうですけど、このあたり……要するに孔子の影響を受けている地域は、男性が女性より優れていると思いがちなんです。それが、あなたがたの歴史であり伝統なので、それを変えるのはとても難しいことです。

　問題は、あなたたちが「人間の平等」についてどう考えているかです。私たちアメリカの憲法では、men（人間、男性）の平等について謳っていて、menやmanという言葉で人類を代表しています。ですから、歴史的には私たちも、女性を劣った存在として見下していたわけです。

　世界は今、変わりつつあります。私たちは、黒人、つまりアフリカからの奴隷に関する歴史について、大変悲しく思っています。女性の権利も、男性の権利に比べる

5 Comfort Women Issue and Women's Rights

compared to men's rights. We, ourselves have reflected about our histories and we just want to teach what we learned from our mistakes to our friends, "You should change your course or your future. This is the right situation or right choice."

Japanese people should use more women power. It's not regarded as very important. Men are not so clever when they are born as men. Also, it's difficult to say, but women are not so inferior to men when we are born. So, I insist that both sexes can have the same quality regarding their jobs and towards the future. This is the new stance of the advanced countries. I think so.

So, Japan should change on the women's position and salary. Even salaries are controlled at a very low level. It is not equal in Japan. But here, in Happy Science, a little different phenomenon can be seen. I don't exactly know the reason.

Saito Even in the political world, our party's top is a woman. So I think we can be good friends.

と非常に低いものでした。私たち自身、自分たちの歴史を反省しましたし、まさに、自分たちの過ちから学んだことを、友人たちに伝えたいと思っています。「あなたたちは、進む道を、未来を変えるべきです。こちらが正しい状態、あるいは正しい選択ですよ」と。

日本人は、もっと女性の力を使うべきです。そこが、あまり重視されていません。男性は、男性として生まれた時点では、それほど賢いわけではありませんし、女性も、言い方は難しいですが、生まれながらにして男性よりそれほど劣っているわけではありません。私が言いたいのは、仕事能力や将来性に関しては、どちらの性も同じだということです。それが、先進国の新しいスタンスだと思います。

ですから、日本は、女性の地位や給料に関して変わるべきです。給料にしても、非常に低いレベルに抑えられていて、日本では平等ではありません。でも、ここ幸福の科学では、少し違う現象が見られるようですね。理由は、はっきりとは分かりませんけど。

斉藤　政治の世界においても、私たちの政党のトップは女性です。ですから、私たちは、良き友人になれると思います。

5 Comfort Women Issue and Women's Rights

She says that she is a sample for raising women's status

Saito We want to make a good situation all over the world. Do you have any plans in Japan aside from what you said about just playing?

Caroline's G.S. Even in America, we don't have women presidents in our history. It's very difficult, even in America, to get the position of president of a huge company or, of course, to change from Mr. President into Mrs. President. It's very difficult in America because men are very strong, usually, and highly educated. Women were permitted to learn like men in these several decades. So, we must catch up to the educational background of men. After that, we must be dealt with equally, I guess. I graduated from Harvard University and Columbia Law School, and I am a lawyer. So, I was appointed as the ambassador. I am one of the samples to you.

5　慰安婦問題と女性の権利について

「私は女性の地位向上のサンプル」

斉藤　私たちは、世界中の状況をよくしたいのです。「遊びに来ただけ」とおっしゃいましたが、それ以外に、日本で何かをする計画は、お持ちでしょうか。

キャロライン守護霊　アメリカでさえ、歴史上、女性の大統領はいません。アメリカでさえ、女性が大企業の社長の地位を得ることや、もちろん、男性の大統領から女性の大統領に変わったりすることは、非常に難しいんです。アメリカでそれが非常に難しいのは、男性は通常、すごく強いですし、高い教育を受けているからです。女性が男性のように学ぶことを許されたのは、ここ数十年のことです。ですから私たちは、男性の学歴に追いつかないといけません。その上で、平等に扱われなければならないのではないでしょうか。私はハーバード大学とコロンビア大学ロースクールを卒業して、弁護士ですので、大使に選ばれました。あなたたちにとって、一つのサンプルです。

5 Comfort Women Issue and Women's Rights

Saito But I think you have another weapon other than being the daughter of JFK or such kind of education.

Caroline's G.S. Another weapon? Maybe the speech ability. Some speak well, and others speak not-so-well. It appears in both sides, men and women. So how about power of speech? That is the new horizon for women to get status, political power and economic power.

Ishikawa You published about ten books, I think.

Caroline's G.S. Yes. Write books, and please make speeches. It's a common road to become great.

Ishikawa Perhaps you were inspired by President Obama's speech.

Caroline's G.S. Inspired by? Sometimes.

斉藤　でも、あなたは、JFKの娘であることや、そういった教育があること以外に、もう一つの〝武器〟をお持ちであると思います。

キャロライン守護霊　もう一つの〝武器〟ですか。たぶん、「スピーチ能力」でしょうか。スピーチが上手な人もいれば、あまり上手でない人もいます。男性と女性の両方ともに見受けられることです。ですから、「スピーチ能力」では、いかがでしょう。それが、女性が地位や政治力や経済力を得るための、新たな地平線です。

石川　あなたは、10冊ほど本を出されていると思います。

キャロライン守護霊　ええ。本を書いて、スピーチをしてください。それが、立派な人間になるための共通の道です。

石川　あなたは、オバマ大統領のスピーチに影響されたのかもしれませんね。

キャロライン守護霊　影響ですか。受けたこともありました。

5 Comfort Women Issue and Women's Rights

Ishikawa OK. I would like to ask about TPP.

Caroline's G.S. TPP? (laughs)

Ishikawa Yes. Sorry. If difficult, a short time...

Caroline's G.S. TPP. OK, OK, OK. TPP. OK, OK, OK. T-P-P.

Ishikawa President Obama delivered his State of the Union Address recently. "New trade partnerships with Asia-Pacific will help them create more jobs." But negotiations...

Caroline's G.S. You speak a lot.

Ishikawa But negotiations of TPP are, as you know,

石川　分かりました。では、TPPについて伺いたいと思います。

キャロライン守護霊　TPPですか（笑）。

石川　ええ。すみません。もし、難しいようでしたら、手短にでも……。

キャロライン守護霊　TPPね、オーケー、オーケー。オーケー。TPPね。オーケー、オーケー、分かりました。T・P・Pでしょ。

石川　オバマ大統領は最近、一般教書演説を行ない、「アジア・太平洋との新たな貿易の連携は、更なる雇用に資する」と述べました。しかし、交渉は……。

キャロライン守護霊　あなた、よくしゃべりますね。

石川　しかし、TPPの交渉は、ご存じのように、計画よ

now behind schedule. President Obama is avoiding taking leadership and initiative. Maybe we need to increase cultural exchanges or economical exchanges.

Caroline's G.S. Because he isn't good at economic policy. He's a good speaker, a religionist-like political speaker. He is good at making religion-like speeches. But he's not so good at understanding economics.

Ishikawa You...

Caroline's G.S. I also don't understand economy.

6 The Reason Behind the Kennedy Tragedies

Wada Going back to our discussion about your father, I'm sorry I have to ask this, but do you know the reason why your father was assassinated?

り遅れています。オバマ大統領は、リーダーシップを取って率先することを避けています。私たちは、もっと文化交流や経済的交易を増やす必要があるかもしれません。

キャロライン守護霊　彼は、あまり経済政策に明るくないからですよ。彼はスピーチは上手で、宗教家のような政治演説をします。宗教のようなスピーチをするのは上手ですけど、経済の理解はあまり明るくないんです。

石川　あなたは……。

キャロライン守護霊　私も、経済は分からないんです。

6　ケネディ家の悲劇の理由

和田　あなたのお父様の話に戻ります。申し訳ないのですが、これをお聞きしなければなりません。お父様が、なぜ暗殺されたのか、理由をご存じでしょうか。

6 The Reason Behind the Kennedy Tragedies

Caroline's G.S. (Sighs) Severe question, also.

Ishikawa There's a conspiracy theory behind his assassination.

Caroline's G.S. Yes, a conspiracy. Yes. Yes. I know, I know.

Ishikawa That he tried to reveal the secrets of Roswell* to the public.

*Secret of Roswell (Roswell Incident): In July 1947, a UFO-like airborne object crashed near Roswell, New Mexico. Apparently, the remains of the object and its crew were captured by the U.S. military. The military stated that they captured a "broken flying disk," but hours later restated that it was a weather balloon. The truth is still unknown.

キャロライン守護霊　（ため息）これも厳しい質問ね。

石川　彼の暗殺の裏には、一つの陰謀説があります。

キャロライン守護霊　ええ、陰謀ね。はい、はい、知ってます、知ってます。

石川　「ロズウェルの秘密（注）を公開しようとしたからだ」というものです。

Air Force officers displayed the remains found near Roswell.

ロズウェル付近で回収した残骸を示す空軍関係者たち。

（注）ロズウェルの秘密（ロズウェル事件）：1947年7月に、ニューメキシコ州のロズウェル付近で、UFOらしき飛行物が墜落し、米軍が機体の残骸と搭乗者の遺体を回収したとされる事件が起きた。米軍はいったん「壊れた空飛ぶ円盤を回収した」と発表したが、数時間後に「気象を観測するための気球だった」と発表を訂正した。真相は現在も不明。

Caroline's G.S. (Laughs) I don't think so. I don't believe so.

Ishikawa Right, it was a little extreme example.

Caroline's G.S. I don't believe so. It's very famous. It's one of the amusements. I'm guessing that he was assassinated by right-wing people, I mean the people who loved to keep the huge military power of the United States and who wanted to continue the Vietnam War. My father... my daddy, was assassinated in 1963, but if he were alive in 1964, the end of the Vietnam War might

キャロライン守護霊　（笑）そうは思いません。そうではないと思います。

石川　ええ、少し極端(きょくたん)な例でしたね。

キャロライン守護霊　そうではないでしょう。すごく有名ですけど、それは興味本位で言ってるだけです。私の推測では、父は、右派の人たち、つまり、米国が巨大な軍事力を持ち続けることやベトナム戦争を続けることを望んでいた人たちによって、暗殺されたのだと思います。父は……パパは1963年に暗殺されましたけれど、もし1964年にも生きていたら、そこでベトナム戦争は終結し

The Vietnam War (early 1960's - 1975)
ベトナム戦争（1960年代初頭開戦 − 1975年終戦）

have come at the time. He was killed in order to continue the Vietnam War till the end of the sixties. Johnson, who at the time was Vice President, became president and continued the Vietnam War for five or six more years. There was pressure by the military industry of America, I think.

Truth Behind the 'Kennedy Curse'

Wada Also, the 'Kennedy Curse,' is a very famous thing. As a spirit, do you think there is a spiritual reason behind members of the Kennedy family dying early?

Caroline's G.S. (Laughs) (taps lap with both hands, twice)

Ishikawa I think maybe late Robert Kennedy…

Caroline's G.S. (Pointing to herself) Next?

(Audience laughs)

たかもしれません。60年代が終わるまでベトナム戦争を続けるために、殺されたんです。当時副大統領だったジョンソンが大統領になって、そこから5、6年、ベトナム戦争を続けたんです。アメリカの軍事産業からの圧力があったのではないかと思います。

「ケネディ家の呪い」の真相

和田 また、「ケネディ家の呪い」というのも非常に有名です。ケネディ家の人たちが早逝することについて、霊人としての立場から、霊的な理由があるとお考えでしょうか。

キャロライン守護霊 （笑）（2回、両手で膝をたたく）

石川 確か、ロバート・ケネディさんは……。

キャロライン守護霊 （自分自身を指して）次ですか。

（会場笑）

Ishikawa Robert Kennedy was also assassinated. And maybe, your younger brother died in a plane crash?

Caroline's G.S. My schedule? You want to know my schedule? When will I be assassinated?

Ishikawa No, no, as a spiritual existence, do you know the truth behind the tragedy?

Caroline's G.S. Tragedy... Oh, you should ask, "Why are you still alive?" That might be a good question.

Why the Kennedys were assassinated, or killed?

6　ケネディ家の悲劇の理由

石川　ロバート・ケネディも暗殺されたと思います。そして、あなたの弟さんは飛行機事故でしたでしょうか。

キャロライン守護霊　私の予定ですか。私の予定を知りたいんですね。私がいつ暗殺されるか。

石川　いえ、いえ、霊的存在として、あなたは悲劇の裏にある真実をご存じなのでしょうか。

キャロライン守護霊　悲劇の……。ああ、「なぜ、あなたはまだ生きているのか」と聞いてもらったほうがいいですね。それなら、いい質問かもしれません。
　なぜ、ケネディ家の人々が暗殺されたか、殺されたか。

Robert Francis Kennedy (1925 -1968)
Younger brother of J. F. Kennedy. He was assassinated during the Democratic presidential nomination campaign.

ロバート・フランシス・ケネディ（1925 – 1968）
J・F・ケネディの実弟。民主党の大統領候補指名選のキャンペーン中に暗殺された。

6 The Reason Behind the Kennedy Tragedies

Because America is a country of democracy. That is partly the meaning of democracy. It's one of the understandings of democracy. Democracy means equal starting point. So, the dynasty of the Kennedys or the recent dynasty of President Bush is not so compatible with American history of democracy.

As you know, when a Japanese ambassador came to the United States, he asked about our first president, Washington: "How are the sons or grandsons of President Washington?" At the time, no one could answer that question. That is the springboard of the American democracy. Such kind of dynasty, I mean king-like connection is not so good in the history of

George Herbert Walker Bush (1924 -) The 41st President of the United States of America. Served from January 1989 to January 1993.

ジョージ・H・W・ブッシュ (1924-) アメリカ合衆国第41代大統領。在任1989年1月 - 1993年1月。

それは、アメリカが民主主義の国だからです。それが、民主主義が意味する一つの側面です。民主主義に対する理解の一つです。民主主義は、「出発点における平等」を意味します。ですから、〝ケネディ王朝〟や、近年の〝ブッシュ大統領による王朝〟というのは、アメリカの民主主義の歴史とは、あまり相いれないものなのです。

ご存じのように、日本の大使が合衆国に赴任したとき、初代のワシントン大統領について、「ワシントン大統領のお子さんやお孫さんは、どうされていますか」と尋ねました。そのとき、誰も答えられませんでした。それが、アメリカ民主主義の出発点なのです。アメリカの歴史からすれば、そういった王朝のようなもの、王家のような縁戚関係は、あまりよいことではありません。ケネディ

George Walker Bush (1946 –)
The 43rd President of the United States of America. Served from January 2001 to January 2009. Eldest son of George H.W. Bush.

ジョージ・W・ブッシュ（1946 –）
アメリカ合衆国第43代大統領。在任2001年1月 – 2009年1月。ジョージ・H・W・ブッシュの長男。

America. So, the Kennedys are envied by other people who want to get political power.

Ishikawa You mean, American people's jealousy is behind the tragedy?

Caroline's G.S. I don't know if it is jealousy or not. But, it's the problem of equality, equality of chance.

Ishikawa Is it the plan of the heavenly world?

Caroline's G.S. I don't know. Heavenly world… (laughs) no, it's a deed of the Godfather in America.

7 Drive-hunt Dolphin Killing, and Japanese vs. American Cultures

Ishikawa Sorry, I would like to ask about dolphin drive-hunting.

家は、政治権力を手にしたい人たちから妬(ねた)ましく思われているのです。

石川　悲劇の裏には、アメリカ人の嫉妬(しっと)があるということですか。

キャロライン守護霊　嫉妬かどうかは分かりませんが、平等の問題です。チャンスの平等です。

石川　それは天上界の計画でしょうか。

キャロライン守護霊　分かりません。天上界ね……（笑）いえ、アメリカの〝ゴッドファーザー〟の仕業ですよ。

7　イルカ漁と日米文化の違(ちが)い

石川　すみません。イルカの追(お)い込(こ)み漁について、お聞きしたいのですが。

(Audience laughs)

Caroline's G.S. (Laughs) Oh… (clicks tongue) my first job in Japan. Famous job (taps head six times with knuckles).

Ishikawa Yes, famous job (laughs). You tweeted that you are deeply concerned by inhumanness of drive-hunt, dolphin killing. So you object to drive-hunt killing of dolphins on humanitarian grounds. I think some people or many people responded, for example, "What about the Atomic Bombing or Agent Orange*?" "Dolphin hunt is a traditional fishing culture." I think dietary culture varies according to local culture. American people eat cows or pigs, and those are also mammals. So what do you think about that? Probably it wasn't an appropriate comment?

Caroline's G.S. In Christian history, in religious

---

*A powerful defoliant sprayed by the U.S. military during the Vietnam War which contained dioxin.

（会場笑）

キャロライン守護霊 （笑）ああ……（舌打ち）私の日本での最初の仕事でした。有名な仕事です（6回、頭をげんこつでたたく）。

石川 そうです、有名なお仕事です（笑）。あなたは、追い込み漁でイルカを殺すことについて、非人道的だとして深く憂慮（ゆうりょ）されているとツイートされました。人道的な観点からイルカの追い込み漁に反対されていますが、たとえば「原爆投下やオレンジ剤（ざい）（注）はどうなんですか」「イルカ漁は、伝統的な漁業文化に基づくものです」といったような反応を示した人たちが、多少は、あるいは大勢いたと思います。食文化は土地の文化によって様々であると思います。アメリカ人も牛や豚（ぶた）などを食べますが、それらも哺乳（ほにゅう）類（るい）です。それについてはどう思われますか。適切なコメントではなかったかもしれませんが。

キャロライン守護霊 キリスト教の歴史では、アメリカ

（注）ベトナム戦争中に米軍が撒いた、ダイオキシンを含む強力な枯葉剤。

7 Drive-hunt Dolphin Killing, and Japanese vs. American Cultures

concept of America or Europe, God made humankind and inspired him or her with the souls that are a part of God. But animals are not inspired, so that is the starting point. Christian people divide humankind and animals. And animals are usually edible by humankind. The reason is because they have no souls in them. Some people think that although they do not have education, some of the animals are intelligent, with high IQ. Dolphins are said to have almost the same or more IQ than monkeys. They are next to humankind and they are thought to have some kind of emotion like humankind, and that is one reason.

Another reason is my husband is Jewish, and as you know, in the "Old Testament," there is a tale of a whale. The tale of Jonah. Jonah was stolen by a great fish. It might be a whale. And, he was alive in the belly of the whale, and his life was saved, and he became one of the prophets in Jewish history. So, Jewish people think that whales are very helpful to God's prophets or angel-like people. And whales and dolphins are

やヨーロッパにおける宗教上の考え方として、神は人間を創り、ご自分の一部である魂(たましい)を人間に吹き込みました。しかし、動物は魂を吹き込まれていません。これが出発点です。キリスト教徒は、人間と動物を分けて考えます。そして、魂を宿していないがゆえに、動物は通常、人間に食べられるものなのです。それに対して、「動物は教育こそ受けていないが、高いIQを持った知性のある動物もいる」と考える人もいます。イルカは、猿(さる)と同じくらいか、猿以上のIQを持っていると言われています。人間に次ぐものであり、人間のように何らかの感情を持っていると考えられていて、それが一つの理由です。

　もう一つの理由としては、私の夫はユダヤ人なのですが、ご存じのように旧約聖書にはクジラの話が出てきます。ヨナの物語です。ヨナは大きな魚に連れ去られます。たぶんクジラのことでしょう。ヨナはクジラのお腹の中で生きていて、命が助かり、ユダヤ史上の預言者の一人になりました。ですからユダヤ人は、クジラは神の預言者や天使のような人にとって非常に有益なものであると思っています。そして、クジラとイルカは、ほとんど同じタイプの動物だ

almost same type of animals, and that is another reason, I guess.

Ishikawa I think whales and dolphins belong to cetaceans.

Caroline's G.S. Yes, mammals...

Ishikawa Yes, same species.

Caroline's G.S. Yes, same species as humankind.

Ishikawa But in 2012 in America, sixty-nine great whales were harvested. So, the same cetacean, but why

ということです。これがもう一つの理由だと思います。

石川　クジラもイルカもクジラ目（もく）に属していたと思います。

キャロライン守護霊　そう、哺乳類で……。

石川　そうです。同じ種ですね。

キャロライン守護霊　そうです、人間と同じ種です。

石川　しかし、2012年にアメリカで、大きなクジラが69頭、水揚（みずあ）げされましたね。同じクジラ目ですが、どうし

Jonah and the Whale by Pieter Lastman (1621)
(Held in the archives of Museum Kunstpalast in Germany)

『ヨナとクジラ』ピーテル・ラストマン作（1621年）
（ドイツ・クンストパラスト美術館所蔵）

7 Drive-hunt Dolphin Killing, and Japanese vs. American Cultures

do you criticize Japan?

Caroline's G.S. (Sighs) It's a cultural tradition, so we cannot understand equally about another situation. We must be tolerant to other countries. But, one of my cousins is the supporter of Sea Shepherd and he is protesting against the trolling of the whales. So, I had some kind of influence from him.

Ishikawa Basically, most Japanese have never eaten dolphins (laughs). No.

Caroline's G.S. Really? Really?

Ishikawa Most Japanese. I have never eaten, either.

Caroline's G.S. Oh, really…

Ishikawa It's not a big topic. Your influence is very big, so I don't think it's appropriate for an ambassador

て日本を批判するのですか。

キャロライン守護霊　（ため息）文化的な伝統なんでしょうが、ほかのところのことは、同じように理解することはできません。私たちは他の国に対しては寛容でなければなりませんね。しかし、私のいとこがシーシェパードの支持者で、捕鯨に反対しているのです。彼の影響をいくらか受けました。

石川　基本的に、ほとんどの日本人はイルカを食べたことがありません（笑）。はい。

キャロライン守護霊　ほんとうですか？　ほんとうに？

石川　ほとんどの日本人は。私も食べたことがありません。

キャロライン守護霊　まあ、ほんとうですか……。

石川　大きな問題ではありません。あなたの影響力は非常に大きいので、大使がそういうことをツイートするこ

to tweet this. Your personal…

Caroline's G.S. I came here to enjoy. So…

Ishikawa It's not an official comment. You tweeted so…

Caroline's G.S. Dolphin, dolphin…

Ishikawa I think it's the difference in culture.

Caroline's G.S. Be friends to dolphins. It's a symbol of peace.

Ishikawa Maybe a symbol of peace, but different in each country.

Caroline's G.S. Dolphins can say something through their voices. And they can have conversations between

とは適切ではないと思います。あなたの個人的な……。

キャロライン守護霊　私は〝楽しむため〟に来ましたので……。

石川　それは公式のコメントではありませんね。あなたが、そのようにツイートしたのは……。

キャロライン守護霊　イルカ、イルカ……。

石川　文化の違いだと思います。

キャロライン守護霊　イルカとは仲良くしてください。平和の象徴ですから。

石川　平和の象徴かもしれませんが、国によって違うかもしれません。

キャロライン守護霊　イルカは、声を出して言葉を発することができます。イルカ同士で会話ができるのです。

them. Some kind of a sonic voice.

Ishikawa Dolphins are very clever. I have seen a dolphin show (laughs).

Apology for the rudeness to the Japanese during World War II
Saito I know you like dolphins, and I know you like Japan. What kind of a topic on Japan do you like?

Caroline's G.S. Topics?

Saito Topics or places.

Caroline's G.S. Hmm. I was asked hundreds of times about that kind of a question. And the official comment on that is, I like Kyoto and Nara (laughs).

(Audience laughs)

一種の音波による声です。

石川　イルカはとても賢いですね。私はイルカショーを見たことがあります（笑）。

第二次大戦中、日本人に無礼をはたらいたことを謝罪

斉藤　あなたがイルカや日本を好きなことは存じ上げていますが、日本について、どのような話題がお好きですか。

キャロライン守護霊　話題ですか。

斉藤　話題、あるいは場所などです。

キャロライン守護霊　うーん。そういう質問は何百回も聞かれました。それに対する公式の答えは、「私は京都や奈良が好きです」（笑）。

（会場笑）

Saito Only places or history?

Caroline's G.S. Huh?

Saito Only places? Or, do you like Japanese history and culture?

Caroline's G.S. Hmm… My honeymoon was in Japan. So, I like Japan and that's a real thing. My father also liked Japan, and Japanese people have been respected in the Kennedy family. We know about that. That is one reason we like Japan, formally. I like Japan, also.

Saito Formally. So informally or privately, do you like Japan?

Caroline's G.S. Hmm. It's only just been two months or so. I want to make my friends here in Japan. And I want to learn a lot about Japanese people, Japanese

斉藤　場所とか歴史だけでしょうか。

キャロライン守護霊　はい？

斉藤　場所だけでしょうか。あるいは、日本の歴史や文化はお好きでしょうか。

キャロライン守護霊　うーん……。私の新婚(しんこん)旅行先は日本でした。ですから、日本が好きというのはほんとうです。父も日本が好きでしたし、ケネディ家では日本人は尊敬されてきました。私たちはそのことを知っています。それが、公式には、私たちが日本好きな理由の一つです。私も日本が好きです。

斉藤　公式には。では、非公式には、あるいは内々には、あなたは日本が好きですか。

キャロライン守護霊　うーん。まだ2ヵ月くらいですので。日本で友人を作りたいと思っています。そして、日本人や日本の歴史、日本の美や芸術、日本人の考え方などを

history, Japanese beauty and arts, and Japanese ways of thinking. And Japanese gods in your history. We want to know a lot. I want to know a lot. I must convey that fact to the nation of the United States. And we must understand, comprehend each other about our culture.

Unfortunately, during the late war period, Japan and the United States misunderstood each other, and we, American people called Japanese people as *Jap* or *yellow monkey* like that. It's very rude of us. We must apologize about that. Japanese people are cleverer than dolphins. So I must insist and confirm about that.

Saito Thank you. So, is there any point that we, Japanese misunderstand you or the U.S. on?

Caroline's G.S. Hmm. America is a very complicated country. It is not made of one nation, I mean one tribe or one color or one religion or one couple of Adam and Eve.

American people are made from a lot of people who

たくさん学びたいと思っています。また、日本の歴史上の神々についても。私たちは、また私は、多くのことを知りたいのです。その内容をアメリカ国民に伝えなければなりません。私たちは、お互（たが）いの文化について分かり合い理解し合う必要があります。

　不幸にも、先の戦争中、日本とアメリカの間に互いに誤解があり、アメリカ人は日本人のことを「ジャップ」とか「イエローモンキー」などと呼んでいました。非常に無礼なことです。それに関しては謝罪しなければいけません。日本人はイルカよりも頭がいいですから。私としては、そのことを強調、確認しておかなければなりません。

斉藤　ありがとうございます。では、私たち日本人が、あなたやアメリカを誤解している点はあるでしょうか。

キャロライン守護霊　うーん。アメリカはとても複雑な国なんです。単一の民族から成り立ってはいません。一つの種族とか、一つの肌（はだ）の色とか、一つの宗教とか、アダムとイブの一組の夫婦といった意味においてです。

　アメリカ人は、いろいろな国に住んでいた、多くの人々

lived in a lot of countries, and we must re-make-up our mind to become American, and love America and love our flag, and fight against the enemies of America. That is the condition of being American people.

You are not so. If you are born in Japan, you are Japanese. Some of you don't respect your *hinomaru*, your flag of the rising sun, but he or she can be a Japanese at the same time. Some fight against enemies of Japan and some hesitate to fight against enemies of Japan. But they can be Japanese. It's a little different.

Plans after ambassador

Ishikawa This is my last question. So, I would like to ask about your personal future plan.

Caroline's G.S. Personal future plan?

Ishikawa Yes. Your future career. For example, in 2008, I think you came close to running for Hillary Clinton's New York senate seat. It was the same one as

から成り立っているので、私たちは「アメリカ人」になろうと決意し直し、アメリカとアメリカ国旗を愛し、「アメリカの敵」と戦わなければいけないのです。それが、アメリカ国民であるための条件です。

　あなたがたは、そうではありません。日本で生まれたら「日本人」です。あなたがたのなかには、日の丸、日章旗に敬意を払わない人もいますが、それでも「日本人」でいられます。「日本の敵」と戦う人もいますし、「日本の敵」と戦うのをためらう人もいますが、それでも「日本人」でいられるのです。少し違いますね。

大使任期後の計画を語る

石川　私から最後の質問です。あなたの個人的な将来の計画について伺いたいのですが。

キャロライン守護霊　個人的な将来の計画ですか。

石川　はい。あなたの将来のキャリアについてです。例えば、2008年、あなたはヒラリー・クリントンの後継のニューヨーク州上院議員選出馬に意欲を見せました。叔

your uncle Robert Kennedy, but he was assassinated. But, I think you…

Caroline's G.S. My assassination plan?

Ishikawa No, no. Not that plan, maybe in three years you will complete your role as ambassador and perhaps you will return to the U.S.

Caroline's G.S. Maybe.

Ishikawa So, in 2008 you tried to run for the New York senate seat, but you quickly withdrew. Do you want to become the senator or the Secretary of State like Hillary Clinton in the future? Or do you expect such things from your children?

Caroline's G.S. I have some… I have some… fascination about the state of… I mean the Hillary experience. Like some kind of a minister regarding

父様であるロバート・ケネディと同じですが、彼は暗殺されました。しかし、あなたは……。

キャロライン守護霊　私の暗殺計画ですか。

石川　いえ、いえ。その計画ではなく、3年後、あなたは大使の任務を終えて、たぶんアメリカに帰国されますよね。

キャロライン守護霊　たぶんね。

石川　2008年にはニューヨーク州上院議員選に出馬しようとされましたが、すぐに取り下げました。あなたは将来、ヒラリー・クリントンのように上院議員や国務長官になりたいのでしょうか。それとも、お子さんたちにそうなってほしいとか。

キャロライン守護霊　私は……私はなんらかの……ヒラリーのような経験には魅力を感じます。なんらかの外交関係の大臣などだと良いですね。ただ、私の〝暗殺計画〟は

foreign problem diplomacy, I hope. But my "assassination program" is not clear, so please ask it to your God. I don't know about that. My father is laughing. If he will invite me in the near future or so, I can't say clearly about that.

Ishikawa Would you want to be a senator?

Caroline's G.S. Hmm… senator. Senator is one choice. And next step, next step will be…

Ishikawa Senator?

Caroline's G.S. Hmm…

Ishikawa How about president?

Caroline's G.S. No, no, no, no, not so. I don't want to be assassinated. I don't want so much. But if possible, I want to have a chance to do something in connection to the foreign policy of the United States. It's good for

不明ですので、あなたがたの神に聞いてください。私には分かりません。父が笑っています、もし父が近い将来にでも私を招くのなら、私は明確なことは言えません。

石川　あなたは上院議員になりたいですか。

キャロライン守護霊　うーん……上院議員。上院議員は一つの選択肢です。そして次のステップ、次はたぶん……。

石川　上院議員？

キャロライン守護霊　うーん……。

石川　大統領はいかがですか。

キャロライン守護霊　いえ、いえ、いえ、いえ。そうは思っていません。私は暗殺されたくありません。そこまで望んではいません。でも、できれば、米国の外交政策関連で何かをするチャンスをいただけたらと思います。それは自分に向い

me. I think so. I have a keen attention about that.

8 Japanese Princess and Roman Emperor in Past Lives?

Saito You said you want to have spiritual connection with Japanese gods. And you like Japan and your father has spiritual connection to Japan, so I would like to ask you about your past life.

Caroline's G.S. Ahh, past life… Formally, we don't have a past life. Personally, hmm, I can guess. Formally, we don't have a past life. But, personally I can guess because I'm staying in Japan. I'm learning Japanese history and I'm learning Japanese Buddhism, so I can guess. I might be a friend of *Amaterasu-O-Mikami**.

Saito Do you have a name that we know?

---

* The supreme goddess in Japanese Shintoism. She lived ca. eighth century B.C. and was born near the modern-day Oita Prefecture. Refer to Chapter Four in *The Golden Laws* (Lantern Books).

ていると思います。その方面には強い関心がありますので。

8　過去世は日本の姫（ひめ）やローマ皇帝（こうてい）か

斉藤　日本の神々と霊的なつながりを持ちたいとおっしゃいましたが、あなたは日本が好きで、お父様も日本に霊的なつながりがあります。ですから、あなたの過去世をお伺いしたいのですが。

キャロライン守護霊　ああ、過去世ですか……。公式には、私たちには過去世はありません。個人的には、うーん、推測はできます。公式には過去世は持っていません。ただ、私は日本に滞在中ですから、個人的に推測はできます。私は日本の歴史を学んでいますし、日本の仏教も学んでいますので、推測できます。もしかしたら天照大神（あまてらすおおみかみ）（注）のお友だちかもしれませんね。

斉藤　私たちが知っているようなお名前がありますか。

（注）日本神道の主宰神。紀元前8世紀頃、現在の大分県のあたりに生まれた。『黄金の法』（幸福の科学出版刊）第4章参照。

151

Caroline's G.S. Hmm, I don't know. But, it might be *nantoka hime* (Princess so-and-so).

(Audience laughs)

Caroline's G.S. *Nantoka hime, nantoka hime, nantoka hime.*

Saito There are many *hime* (princesses) in Japan.

Ishikawa Princess of the Imperial family or Empress?

Caroline's G.S. Hmm… I'm learning Japanese history so… I guess, I guess, I guess, if I had a past life, I was born in the Edo period and married a Japanese shogun.

Ishikawa Which shogun?

Caroline's G.S. Please choose a suitable one.

8　過去世は日本の姫やローマ皇帝か

キャロライン守護霊　うーん、分かりませんが、もしかしたら、ナントカ姫かもしれません。

（会場笑）

キャロライン守護霊　ナントカ姫、ナントカ姫、ナントカ姫。

斉藤　日本には姫がたくさんいますので。

石川　天皇の内親王ですか。あるいは皇后？

キャロライン守護霊　うーん……私は日本史を学んでいますので……たぶん、たぶん、たぶん、もし過去世があるとしたら、江戸時代に生まれて日本の将軍と結婚しました。

石川　どの将軍ですか。

キャロライン守護霊　いい人を選んでください。

(Audience laughs)

Saito *Go-hime?**

Caroline's G.S. *Go-hime*, sounds good. Nice!

(Audience laughs)

Caroline's G.S. *Go-hime*. Go! Hime! Sounds nice. I like it. Oh, I decided I was *Go-hime*.

(Audience laughs)

Ishikawa Is it true?

Caroline's G.S. I don't know, but it's easy to say (laughs).

---

* The wife of Tokugawa Hidetada who became the second Tokugawa shogun, and the mother of Tokugawa Iemitsu who became the third shogun (1573-1626).

(会場笑)

斉藤　江(ごう)姫？（注）

キャロライン守護霊　「Goヒメ」、いい響(ひび)きですね。素敵です！

(会場笑)

キャロライン守護霊　Goヒメ。Go!姫！　いい響きですね。気に入りました。ああ、江姫だったことに決めました。

(会場笑)

石川　ほんとうですか。

キャロライン守護霊　分かりませんが、言い易いので(笑)。

（注）江戸幕府第二代将軍・秀忠の正室、第三代将軍・家光の母（1573-1626）。

8 Japanese Princess and Roman Emperor in Past Lives?

Ishikawa Do you know Iemitsu or Hidetada? Or Yoshimune?*

Caroline's G.S. Iemitsu, Hidetada, Yoshimune. Iemitsu, Hidetada. Iemitsu, Hidetada. Iemitsu, Hidetada, Iemitsu, Hidetada. Iemitsu, Hidetada, Iemitsu, Hidetada, Iemitsu, Iemitsu, Hidetada, Iemitsu, Iemitsu, Iemitsu, Hidetada, Iemitsu.

Ishikawa Iemitsu is the third Tokugawa shogun.

Caroline's G.S. Is he clever or not?

---

* Tokugawa Iemitsu (Image above: 1604-1651) : The third shogun of the Tokugawa shogunate. He was the second son of Hidetada.
Tokugawa Hidetada (1579-1632) : The second shogun of the Tokugawa shogunate. He was the third son of Tokugawa Ieyasu, the first shogun of the Tokugawa shogunate.
Tokugawa Yoshimune(1684-1751) : The eighth shogun of the Tokugawa shogunate.

8 過去世は日本の姫やローマ皇帝か

石川　家光や秀忠はご存じですか。あるいは吉宗は。（注）

キャロライン守護霊　家光、秀忠、吉宗。家光、秀忠。家光、秀忠。家光、秀忠、家光、秀忠。家光、秀忠、家光、秀忠、家光、家光、秀忠、家光、家光、家光、秀忠、家光。

石川　家光は徳川第三代将軍です。

キャロライン守護霊　賢い人ですか、違いますか。

(注)　徳川家光（肖像画。1604-1651）江戸幕府第三代将軍。秀忠の二男。
　　　徳川秀忠（1579-1632）江戸幕府第二代将軍。初代将軍・家康の三男。
　　　徳川吉宗（1684-1751）江戸幕府第八代将軍。

Ishikawa Yes, I think he's clever.

Caroline's G.S. Clever? Ah, OK then, Iemitsu.

(Audience laughs)

Ishikawa Iemitsu's daughter? Or Iemitsu's wife?

Caroline's G.S. Ah, daughter or wife? Hmm, daughter or wife.

Saito Could you tell us the truth?

Caroline's G.S. Formally, we don't have a past life.

Ishikawa Yes, we know.

Caroline's G.S. You know? This is a fantasy. Ah, I'm a fantasy teller as a Japan-staying ambassador. I imagine,

8　過去世は日本の姫やローマ皇帝か

石川　ええ、賢いと思いますよ。

キャロライン守護霊　賢い？　ああ、OK、では家光です。

（会場笑）

石川　家光の娘ですか。それとも家光の妻ですか。

キャロライン守護霊　ああ、娘か妻か。うーん、娘か妻か。

斉藤　真実を教えてくださいませんか。

キャロライン守護霊　公式には、私たちには過去世はありません。

石川　はい、分かっています。

キャロライン守護霊　でしょう？　これは空想です。ああ、私は駐日(ちゅうにち)大使として、ファンタジーを語るわけですよ。

maybe Iemitsu's wife. One of the wives.

Ishikawa Oh, I see.

One of the Five Good Emperors

Saito Could you tell us the story of another one?

Caroline's G.S. Another fantasy?

Saito Another fantasy.

Caroline's G.S. Another fantasy, another fantasy, another fantasy, maybe, ah, another fantasy, maybe Europe. Europe.

Ishikawa Which country?

Caroline's G.S. Maybe, Rome? Rome, I guess.

想像するに、家光の妻かもしれません。妻の一人です。

石川　ああ、分かりました。

ローマ五賢帝の一人か
斉藤　ほかに教えていただける過去世はありますか。

キャロライン守護霊　ほかのファンタジー？

斉藤　ほかのファンタジーです。

キャロライン守護霊　ほかのファンタジー、ほかのファンタジー、ほかのファンタジー。たぶん、ああ、ほかのファンタジーは、たぶんヨーロッパです。ヨーロッパ。

石川　どちらの国ですか。

キャロライン守護霊　たぶん、ローマかしら。ローマだと思います。

Ishikawa Famous emperor's wife or daughter?

Caroline's G.S. It's your option. Formally, we don't have a past life, so it's your option. Please decide or recommend it to me. At that time, I'm not female. I must be a male. I used to be a male. Some kind of inspiration… one of the Roman emperors. Some inspiration came from Heaven and said so.

Saito Could you tell us the name?

Caroline's G.S. Name?

Saito The name. The name of the emperor.

Caroline's G.S. Maybe this inspiration comes from a Japanese person who knows the history of the world. I don't know who he is, but he said that it's Emperor Trajan, like that.

石川　有名な皇帝の妻か娘ですか。

キャロライン守護霊　あなたがたが選んでください。公式には、私たちには過去世はありませんので、あなたがたの選択です。決めるか、私に勧(すす)めてください。その時代には女性ではありません。男性だったはずです。男性でした。何かインスピレーションが……ローマ皇帝の一人です。天国から何かインスピレーションがきて、そう言いました。

斉藤　そのお名前を教えていただけますか。

キャロライン守護霊　名前？

斉藤　名前です、その皇帝の名前を。

キャロライン守護霊　これはたぶん、世界史を知っている日本人から来たインスピレーションですね。彼が誰なのかは分かりませんが、彼は、トラヤヌス帝(てい)だというようなことを言いました。

Ishikawa Really?

Caroline's G.S. I don't know. I don't know exactly.

Ishikawa One of the Five Good Emperors.

Caroline's G.S. Yes, yes, he said so. But if it's true or not, I don't know clearly. Might be entertainment.

石川　ほんとうですか。

キャロライン守護霊　分かりません。正確には分かりません。

石川　有名な五賢帝のうちの一人ですね。

キャロライン守護霊　はい、はい、彼はそう言いました、ただ、ほんとうかどうか、はっきりとは分かりません。もしかしたらエンタテインメントかも。

Emperor Trajan
(Marcus Ulpius Nerva Trajanus Augustus)
One of the Five Good Emperors of the Roman Empire. Reigned from 98 A.D. to 117 A.D.

トラヤヌス帝
（マルクス・ウルピウス・ネルウァ・トラヤヌス・アウグストゥス）
ローマ帝国の皇帝。五賢帝の一人。在位98年－117年。

9 Message to Japan

Ishikawa Thank you so much. We hope that you will serve as a fine bridge between two countries. Thank you so much.

Caroline's G.S. Oh, thank you. Is there any other question?

Wada Then, finally, would you like to give a message to Japanese and American people?

Caroline's G.S.
> Love Japan.
> Love the United States.
> And next, love the world.
> Don't be serious about the conflicts between you and Korea, or you and China.
> We will persuade them. So, don't be serious.
> Rely on us.

9　日本へのメッセージ

石川　どうもありがとうございました。私たちは、あなたが両国の素晴らしい架け橋として務められることを望んでいます。どうもありがとうございました。

キャロライン守護霊　ああ、ありがとう。ほかに何か質問はありますか。

和田　では、最後に、日本人とアメリカ人に向けたメッセージをいただけますか。

キャロライン守護霊
　日本を愛してください。
　米国を愛してください。
　そして次には、世界を愛してください。
　韓国や中国との争いに深刻になりすぎないでください。
　私たちが彼らを説得します。ですから深刻にならず、
　私たちを頼りにしてください。

Is this OK?

Ishikawa Thank you so much.

This interview will be a springboard to the Political Field

Ryuho Okawa Thank you (claps hands and ends session). Hmm. How was it?

Ishikawa I think it might be that she still needs experience and knowledge. I don't think she has a clear vision or policy.

Ryuho Okawa She doesn't have enough power to decide the foreign policy toward Japan. In America, there is a bureaucracy of foreign ministry and the existence of Mr. Obama. She's one of the speakers for them.

Ishikawa I think she's very close to President Obama and the Secretary of State John Kerry.

これでいいですか。

石川　ありがとうございました。

このインタビューが政治でのスプリングボードに

大川隆法　ありがとうございました（手を叩いて霊言を終える）。うーん、どうでしたか。

石川　彼女は、まだ経験や知識が足りていないのかなと思います。明確なビジョンやポリシーがないように思いました。

大川隆法　日本との外交に関して、十分な決定権は持っていませんからね。アメリカでは外交官僚とオバマさんの存在がありますので。彼女は、そのスピーカーの一人ですから。

石川　オバマ大統領やジョン・ケリー国務長官と非常に近いと思います。

Ryuho Okawa Yes. Yes.

Ishikawa I think, basically, her policy depends on their stance. If Hillary Clinton was the Secretary of State, maybe her stance might have been stronger. I think.

Ryuho Okawa This is her springboard to the political field. I think so. Thank you very much.

大川隆法　はい、そうですね。

石川　基本的には、彼女のポリシーは彼らのスタンスによると思います。もしヒラリー・クリントンが国務長官だったら、彼女のスタンスも、もっと強くなっていたかもしれないと思います。

大川隆法　これは彼女にとって、政治の分野に向けたスプリングボードになると思います。どうもありがとうございました。

『守護霊インタビュー 駐日アメリカ大使
キャロライン・ケネディ 日米の新たな架け橋』
大川隆法著作関連書籍

『ヒラリー・クリントンの政治外交リーディング』
（幸福実現党刊）

『「河野談話」「村山談話」を斬る！』
（幸福の科学出版刊）

『従軍慰安婦問題と南京大虐殺は本当か？』
（幸福の科学出版刊）

『神に誓って「従軍慰安婦」は実在したか』
（幸福実現党刊）

『安重根は韓国の英雄か、それとも悪魔か』
（幸福の科学出版刊）

『潘基文国連事務総長の守護霊インタビュー』
（幸福の科学出版刊）

『バラク・オバマのスピリチュアル・メッセージ』
（幸福の科学出版刊）

『原爆投下は人類への罪か？』（幸福実現党刊）

『マッカーサー戦後65年目の証言』（幸福の科学出版刊）

守護霊インタビュー　駐日アメリカ大使キャロライン・ケネディ
日米の新たな架け橋

2014年2月20日　初版第1刷

著　者　　大　川　隆　法

発行所　　幸福の科学出版株式会社

〒107-0052　東京都港区赤坂2丁目10番14号
TEL(03)5573-7700
http://www.irhpress.co.jp/

印刷・製本　　株式会社 堀内印刷所

落丁・乱丁本はおとりかえいたします
©Ryuho Okawa 2014. Printed in Japan. 検印省略
ISBN978-4-86395-441-0 C0030
Photo：時事通信フォト /dpa/ 時事通信フォト /AFP＝時事 /The Bridgeman Art Library/
AP/ アフロ /Everett/Collection/ZUMA Press

大川隆法ベストセラーズ・この一冊で、もっと強くなれる

忍耐の法
「常識」を逆転させるために

法シリーズ第20作

人生のあらゆる苦難を乗り越え、夢や志を実現させる方法が、この一冊に。

混迷の現代を生きるすべての人に贈る待望の「法シリーズ」第20作！

2,000円

第1章	スランプの乗り切り方	── 運勢を好転させたいあなたへ
第2章	試練に打ち克つ	── 後悔しない人生を生き切るために
第3章	徳の発生について	── 私心を去って「天命」に生きる
第4章	敗れざる者	── この世での勝ち負けを超える生き方
第5章	常識の逆転	── 新しい時代を拓く「真理」の力

幸福の科学出版

大川隆法ベストセラーズ・英語説法&最新英語霊言

Power to the Future
未来に力を

英語説法集 日本語訳付き

予断を許さない日本の国防危機。混迷を極める世界情勢の行方――。ワールド・ティーチャーが英語で語った、この国と世界の進むべき道とは。

1,400円

守護霊インタビュー
タイ・インラック首相から日本へのメッセージ

英語霊言 日本語訳付き

民主化を妨げる伝統仏教の弊害。イスラム勢力による紛争。中国の脅威――。政治的混乱に苦しむインラック首相守護霊からのメッセージとは。

1,400円

ネルソン・マンデラ
ラスト・メッセージ

英語霊言 日本語訳付き

人種差別と戦い、27年もの投獄に耐え、民族融和の理想を貫いた偉大なる指導者ネルソン・マンデラ。その「復活」のメッセージを全世界の人びとに!

1,400円

※表示価格は本体価格(税別)です。

大川隆法 ベストセラーズ・世界の指導者の本心

バラク・オバマの スピリチュアル・メッセージ
再選大統領は世界に平和をもたらすか

弱者救済と軍事費削減、富裕層への増税……。再選翌日のオバマ大統領守護霊インタビューを緊急刊行！日本の国防危機が明らかになる。
【幸福実現党刊】

英語霊言 日本語訳付き

1,400円

ヒラリー・クリントンの 政治外交リーディング
同盟国から見た日本外交の問題点

竹島、尖閣と続発する日本の領土問題……。国防意識なき同盟国をアメリカはどう見ているのか？ クリントン国務長官の本心に迫る！
【幸福実現党刊】

1,400円

マッカーサー 戦後65年目の証言
マッカーサー・吉田茂・山本五十六・鳩山一郎の霊言

GHQ最高司令官・マッカーサーの霊によって、占領政策の真なる目的が明かされる。日本の大物政治家、連合艦隊司令長官の霊言も収録。

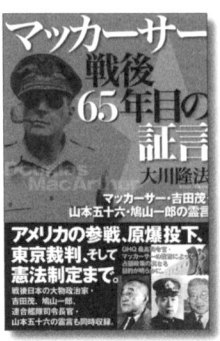

1,200円

幸福の科学出版

大川隆法ベストセラーズ・世界の指導者の本心

中国と習近平に未来はあるか
反日デモの謎を解く

「反日デモ」も、「反原発・沖縄基地問題」も中国が仕組んだ日本占領への布石だった。緊迫する日中関係の未来を習近平氏守護霊に問う。
【幸福実現党刊】

1,400円

潘基文(バンキムン)国連事務総長の守護霊インタビュー

「私が考えているのは、韓国の利益だけだ。次は、韓国の大統領になる」──。国連トップ・潘氏守護霊が明かす、その驚くべき本心とは。

英語霊言
日本語訳付き

1,400円

ロシア・プーチン 新大統領と帝国の未来
守護霊インタヴュー

中国が覇権主義を拡大させるなか、ロシアはどんな国家戦略をとるのか!? また、親日家プーチン氏の意外な過去世も明らかに。
【幸福実現党刊】

1,300円

※表示価格は本体価格(税別)です。

大川隆法 霊言シリーズ・正しい歴史認識のために

従軍慰安婦問題と南京大虐殺は本当か？
左翼の源流 vs. E.ケイシー・リーディング

「従軍慰安婦問題」も「南京事件」も中国や韓国の捏造だった！ 日本の自虐史観や反日主義の論拠が崩れる、驚愕の史実が明かされる。

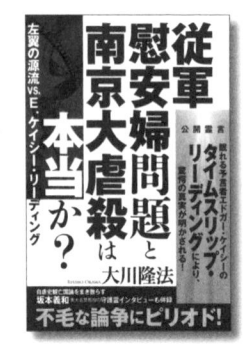

1,400円

神に誓って「従軍慰安婦」は実在したか

いまこそ、「歴史認識」というウソの連鎖を断つ！ 元従軍慰安婦を名乗る2人の守護霊インタビューを刊行！ 慰安婦問題に隠された驚くべき陰謀とは!?
【幸福実現党刊】

1,400円

安重根は韓国の英雄か、それとも悪魔か
安重根 & 朴槿惠(パク クネ)大統領守護霊の霊言

なぜ韓国は、中国にすり寄るのか？ 従軍慰安婦の次は、安重根像の設置を打ち出す朴槿惠・韓国大統領の恐るべき真意が明らかに。

1,400円

幸福の科学出版

大川隆法 霊言シリーズ・正しい歴史認識のために

公開霊言 東條英機、「大東亜戦争の真実」を語る

戦争責任、靖国参拝、憲法改正……。
他国からの不当な内政干渉にモノ言えぬ日本。正しい歴史認識を求めて、東條英機が先の大戦の真相を語る。
【幸福実現党刊】

1,400円

原爆投下は人類への罪か?
公開霊言 トルーマン＆F・ルーズベルトの新証言

なぜ、終戦間際に、アメリカは日本に2度も原爆を落としたのか?「憲法改正」を語る上で避けては通れない難題に「公開霊言」が挑む。
【幸福実現党刊】

1,400円

「河野談話」「村山談話」を斬る!
日本を転落させた歴史認識

根拠なき歴史認識で、これ以上日本が謝る必要などない!! 守護霊インタビューで明らかになった、驚愕の新証言。「大川談話（私案）」も収録。

1,400円

※表示価格は本体価格（税別）です。

幸福の科学グループのご案内

宗教、教育、政治、出版などの活動を通じて、地球的ユートピアの実現を目指しています。

宗教法人　幸福の科学

1986年に立宗。1991年に宗教法人格を取得。信仰の対象は、地球系霊団の最高大霊、主エル・カンターレ。世界100カ国以上の国々に信者を持ち、全人類救済という尊い使命のもと、信者は、「愛」と「悟り」と「ユートピア建設」の教えの実践、伝道に励んでいます。

（2014年2月現在）

愛

幸福の科学の「愛」とは、与える愛です。これは、仏教の慈悲や布施の精神と同じことです。信者は、仏法真理をお伝えすることを通して、多くの方に幸福な人生を送っていただくための活動に励んでいます。

悟り

「悟り」とは、自らが仏の子であることを知るということです。教学や精神統一によって心を磨き、智慧を得て悩みを解決すると共に、天使・菩薩の境地を目指し、より多くの人を救える力を身につけていきます。

ユートピア建設

私たち人間は、地上に理想世界を建設するという尊い使命を持って生まれてきています。社会の悪を押しとどめ、善を推し進めるために、信者はさまざまな活動に積極的に参加しています。

海外支援・災害支援

国内外の世界で貧困や災害、心の病で苦しんでいる人々に対しては、現地メンバーや支援団体と連携して、物心両面にわたり、あらゆる手段で手を差し伸べています。

自殺を減らそうキャンペーン

年間約3万人の自殺者を減らすため、全国各地で街頭キャンペーンを展開しています。

公式サイト www.withyou-hs.net

ヘレンの会

ヘレン・ケラーを理想として活動する、ハンディキャップを持つ方とボランティアの会です。視聴覚障害者、肢体不自由な方々に仏法真理を学んでいただくための、さまざまなサポートをしています。

公式サイト www.helen-hs.net

INFORMATION

お近くの精舎・支部・拠点など、お問い合わせは、こちらまで！
幸福の科学サービスセンター
TEL. **03-5793-1727**（受付時間 火～金:10～20時／土・日:10～18時）
宗教法人 幸福の科学公式サイト **happy-science.jp**

教育

学校法人 幸福の科学学園

学校法人 幸福の科学学園は、幸福の科学の教育理念のもとにつくられた教育機関です。人間にとって最も大切な宗教教育の導入を通じて精神性を高めながら、ユートピア建設に貢献する人材輩出を目指しています。

幸福の科学学園

中学校・高等学校（那須本校）
2010年4月開校・栃木県那須郡（男女共学・全寮制）
TEL **0287-75-7777**
公式サイト **happy-science.ac.jp**

関西中学校・高等学校（関西校）
2013年4月開校・滋賀県大津市（男女共学・寮及び通学）
TEL **077-573-7774**
公式サイト **kansai.happy-science.ac.jp**

幸福の科学大学（仮称・設置認可申請予定）
2015年開学予定
TEL **03-6277-7248**（幸福の科学 大学準備室）
公式サイト **university.happy-science.jp**

仏法真理塾「サクセスNo.1」 TEL **03-5750-0747**（東京本校）
小・中・高校生が、信仰教育を基礎にしながら、「勉強も『心の修行』」と考えて学んでいます。

不登校児支援スクール「ネバー・マインド」 TEL **03-5750-1741**
心の面からのアプローチを重視して、不登校の子供たちを支援しています。
また、障害児支援の「**ユー・アー・エンゼル！**」運動も行っています。

エンゼルプランV TEL **03-5750-0757**
幼少時からの心の教育を大切にして、信仰をベースにした幼児教育を行っています。

シニア・プラン21 TEL **03-6384-0778**
希望に満ちた生涯現役人生のために、年齢を問わず、多くの方が学んでいます。

NPO活動支援

学校からのいじめ追放を目指し、さまざまな社会提言をしています。また、各地でのシンポジウムや学校への啓発ポスター掲示等に取り組むNPO「いじめから子供を守ろう！ネットワーク」を支援しています。

公式サイト **mamoro.org**
ブログ **mamoro.blog86.fc2.com**
相談窓口 **TEL.03-5719-2170**

政治

幸福実現党

内憂外患(ないゆうがいかん)の国難に立ち向かうべく、2009年5月に幸福実現党を立党しました。創立者である大川隆法党総裁の精神的指導のもと、宗教だけでは解決できない問題に取り組み、幸福を具体化するための力になっています。

党員の機関紙「幸福実現NEWS」

TEL 03-6441-0754
公式サイト hr-party.jp

出版メディア事業

大川隆法著作シリーズ

幸福の科学出版

大川隆法総裁の仏法真理の書を中心に、ビジネス、自己啓発、小説など、さまざまなジャンルの書籍・雑誌を出版しています。他にも、映画事業、文学・学術発展のための振興事業、テレビ・ラジオ番組の提供など、幸福の科学文化を広げる事業を行っています。

アー・ユー・ハッピー?
are-you-happy.com

ザ・リバティ
the-liberty.com

幸福の科学出版
TEL 03-5573-7700
公式サイト irhpress.co.jp

入会のご案内

あなたも、幸福の科学に集い、ほんとうの幸福を見つけてみませんか？

幸福の科学では、大川隆法総裁が説く仏法真理をもとに、「どうすれば幸福になれるのか、また、他の人を幸福にできるのか」を学び、実践しています。

入会

大川隆法総裁の教えを信じ、学ぼうとする方なら、どなたでも入会できます。入会された方には、『入会版「正心法語」』が授与されます。（入会の奉納は1,000円目安です）

ネットでも入会できます。詳しくは、下記URLへ。
happy-science.jp/joinus

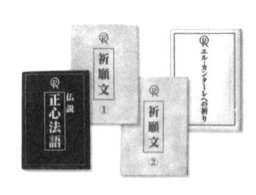

三帰誓願（さんきせいがん）

仏弟子としてさらに信仰を深めたい方は、仏・法・僧の三宝への帰依を誓う「三帰誓願式」を受けることができます。三帰誓願者には、『仏説・正心法語』『祈願文①』『祈願文②』『エル・カンターレへの祈り』が授与されます。

植福の会（しょくふくのかい）

植福は、ユートピア建設のために、自分の富を差し出す尊い布施の行為です。布施の機会として、毎月1口1,000円からお申込みいただける、「植福の会」がございます。

「植福の会」に参加された方のうちご希望の方には、幸福の科学の小冊子（毎月1回）をお送りいたします。詳しくは、下記の電話番号までお問い合わせください。

月刊「幸福の科学」
ザ・伝道
ヤング・ブッダ
ヘルメス・エンゼルズ

INFORMATION

幸福の科学サービスセンター
TEL. 03-5793-1727 （受付時間 火〜金:10〜20時／土・日:10〜18時）
宗教法人 幸福の科学 公式サイト **happy-science.jp**